AWAKEN YOUR PSYCHIC ABILITIES

MARIE HARRIETTE KAY

BALBOA.
PRESS
A DIVISION OF HAY HOUSE

ISBN: 978-1-4525-4645-2 (sc)
ISBN: 978-1-4525-4643-8 (hc)
ISBN: 978-1-4525-4644-5 (e)

Library of Congress Control Number: 2012901285

Balboa Press books may be ordered through booksellers or by contacting:

Balboa Press
A Division of Hay House
1663 Liberty Drive
Bloomington, IN 47403
www.balboapress.com
1-(877) 407-4847

Printed in the United States of America

Balboa Press rev. date: 4/17/2012

DEDICATION

I offer my love and heartfelt thanks to my mother, Eva Kay, who, while in spirit, encouraged and guided me in my spiritual endeavor.

I thank my teacher, June Black, who guided me though seven years of spiritual and psychic training, and I thank her for awakening me to the world of the paranormal.

I thank my three children, Jane, Robert, and Steven, for their encouragement, help, and support while I wrote this book.

Most of all, I thank God for the privilege of teaching others about the spirit world.

REVIEWS

"Marie Kay's book presents meditations, workshops with step-by-step exercises, and spiritual knowledge that will transform your life in a positive way."

—Kathy Nahtygal, healer and psychic

"I have taught groups with the exercises and meditations from *Awaken Your Psychic Abilities* for three years. Most beginners sensed, heard, or saw, within their mind's eye, and experienced spiritual guidance shortly after using these simple techniques. This book has significantly changed the lives of many people, including myself."

—Susi Walter, Founder of Intuitive Endeavors,
Meditation on the Go! (www.susiwalter.com)

"Marie Kay shares with the reader many ways we can open and enhance our spiritual gifts. She is an outstanding spiritual teacher and guide. Be prepared to expand your intuitive abilities and walk the spiritual path."

—Dr. Eric Alsterberg, PhD, psychologist and spiritual author

TABLE OF CONTENTS

FOREWORD

Awaken Your Psychic Abilities is an easy-to-use handbook, whether you're learning to develop your psychic awareness for the first time or you are interested in teaching others. The following material and spiritual knowledge is beneficial to anyone who is interested in learning how to tap into their natural intelligence and awaken their spirituality.

You can expect positive results with each consecutive chapter as you test your own skills. Whether you are in a small group or by yourself, you will learn to see and feel an aura, see images within the mind's eye, and communicate with your spirit guides, angels, and the spirit world. You will acquire the ability to sense negative and/or positive energy and use the power of your mind to a finer degree. If you are teacher or even a novice, the end result will be an increase in your natural intuitive intelligence and your psychic abilities. This will lead to a more peaceful existence in your daily life. The following meditation and exercises have been tried and proven to be effective in the enlightenment of the God consciousness.

All references to God represent an understanding of a universal consciousness—an energy force that unites all people, alive and in spirit, in interconnected love.

Chapter 1

AWAKEN YOUR PSYCHIC ABILITY

Many people have paranormal experiences but don't know why such experiences happen to them. They don't know who to tell or what questions to ask. Besides, who would believe them, anyway? So, instead of searching for an answer, they deny the truth of their own experience. They dismiss it as if it had never happened. If this has happened to you, you're not alone. Many people are intuitive but don't know how to use their ability. Intuition is a natural ability and can be developed just as any profession can benefit from higher learning.

The following material is designed to awaken your spiritual awareness and strengthen your psychic abilities. Whether you want to teach psychic awareness or you are just a beginner, this book is for you. Each chapter offers hands-on exercises that are entertaining and can be completed easily by following the step-by-step instructions. Thirteen detailed meditations and fifteen group exercises are designed to develop different psychic abilities and awaken spiritual awareness. The chapters are presented in a specific order to support the following exercises. Group participation is required to perform most of the exercises. So, gather a group of like-minded friends and neighbors to begin the adventure of becoming psychic.

Class Setup

Five or more people are required to begin your psychic development group. It's important that each person maintains a high level of spiritual intention and purity of thought. Don't use your psychic abilities negatively or to attain power, for they will draw negative energy with disappointing results. Use wisdom in selecting group members. If the group doesn't feel comfortable or fails to meet your spiritual expectations, don't hesitate to leave. Select members who have the same spiritual intentions you wish to attain. The saying *"birds of a feather flock together"* is a good rule by which to set your goals. As you develop spiritually, you may decide to add new members or even change groups. Allow your intuition to guide you. By joining with like-minded people, you will find like-minded psychic development. With practice, you will awaken your spiritual awareness, strengthen your psychic abilities, and become aware of your spirit guides and guardian angels.

Meditation
All meditations used are primers for spiritual awareness. They are designed to create a connection to your higher self, to God, and to the spiritual realm. To be spiritually aware does not depend upon devotion to any specific master, creed, or religion. Meditation is a method by which one focuses from within, usually for the purpose of spiritual enlightenment. A famous psychic named Edgar Cayce said, "Through prayer we speak to God. In meditation, God speaks to us." Cayce was born in Kentucky in 1877. He had the ability to psychically read another person's body and to advise a holistic method to heal the body. Cayce was known to have recorded the most psychic readings of any one person.

The first step to becoming psychic is to learn how to meditate, how meditation affects your physical body, and how meditation awakens psychic awareness. Meditation is a method by which you can relax the mind and body, as well as slow down the brain waves at will. Each new meditation will stimulates the brain to create new circuits. This, in turn, will broaden your attention span, increase alertness, elevate intelligence, enhance creativity, improve health, and bring an awareness of the God consciousness. Meditation reduces stress and leads to a positive change in attitude so daily chores can be performed more easily. As the chapters proceed, the meditations will increase in complexity to awaken psychic abilities.

Brain Communication

Each meditation and psychic exercise is intended to strengthen the intuitive, right side of the brain. The brain is separated into two distinct parts—left brain and right brain. They link in communication.

The left brain is clinical. It receives messages through taste, touch, smell, sight, and sound. Through those senses, the left brain sorts out details, organizes them logically, and acts upon those facts. It counts numbers, keeps time, plans, and draws conclusions. The left brain is the verbal side of the brain related to language, logic, and analysis.

The right brain is intuitive. It's better at spatial concepts. It visualizes images while it solves a problem. It uses symbols, not words, while forming a total picture. The right brain creates, dreams, and imagines. The purpose of meditation is to activate the intuitive, right side of the brain, and to strengthen one's extrasensory perception (ESP).

The nervous system crosses from the right side of the brain to the left hand and from the left side of the brain to the right hand. Left-handed people may be more inclined to be right-brained; therefore, they may use their intuition more readily. Additional information of the third eye will be presented as it applies to its use.

By discussing the following checklist, each person may add additional information. All information is knowledge.

Group Discussion Checklist

Are you logical, left-brained? Do you think with numbers, dates, times, and logic?

Are you intuitive, right-brained? Do you often use your instinct? If so, share your experiences.

If left-handed, are you creative, intuitive, or psychic?

What experience has opened your awareness to the paranormal?

Psychic Energy

You have the ability to create psychic energy. The mere act of several people meditating produces waves of energy that heighten one's psychic awareness. The larger the group, ideally ten or more, the more energy created. The group's combined energy will be used to conduct psychic exercises, such as seeing an aura or feeling a spirit. The greater the energy, the easier it will be to perform the exercises. Psychic energy is also created by the group's spiritual thoughts, intentions, and sincerity. Additional energy is created by each person's angels, spirit guides, a person's personal spirit guides, and totems. Totems are animal guides and protectors for humans. Those who are naturally psychic and/or spiritually aware naturally generate additional energy. Natural healers are a natural channel for energy. They bring powerful energy to the group. A novice will create energy according to his or her auric energy and spiritual awareness.

Positive thoughts also create positive energy. However, energy can be temporarily drained from the group by negative thoughts or by a person who is in need of healing. It's important to be healthy in body and mind in order to maintain a positive flow of energy. Positive energy raises the group's vibrations to a finer degree, thus increasing each person's intuitive ability.

How to Create Protection

Each exercise should begin with a focus on protection. The purpose of protection is to draw spiritual guidance to the group, create positive energy, and nullify negative energy. The most common way to activate protection is to mentally create a God light energy and then mentally project that light around the body.

Prayer is another source of protection. A prayer expressed with sincerity creates positive energy and nullifies negative energy. Before each meditation, the group should either pray or request their angels or guides to stand by for "protection, guidance, and directions." By performing the following exercises in the order presented, you can develop the ability to sense and even see your guides while in meditation; communicate with them in prayer, dreams, or thought; and learn to recognize their guidance. Maintaining the sincere desire to achieve spiritual awareness draws angels and guides closer. Sometimes spirits or angels can be seen or sensed in the mind's eye as they form a protective circle around the group during meditation.

The following short meditation is intended to create God light protection. If you are only one person using this book, you may choose to make a recording of this meditation ahead of time and then follow the meditation. Or if in a group, one person may recite it slowly and softly. For the purpose of all meditations, the ellipsis mark [...] is used to prompt you to slow down before continuing. The pause is used to allow time to absorb the words. Additional commas have been added to clarify the meaning. Meditation music may be played softly but is not required.

Meditation to Create God Light Protection

"Close your eyes. Visualize a white light. Feeling very ... very peaceful as the white light slowly wraps around your body. (Pause.) Slowly take a deep breath, drawing in the God light. As you exhale, allow the light to flow through your body. You're breathing slowly ... deeply. Breathing in the God light. Use your mind to breathe the light outward, until it surrounds your body. (Pause.) This is your God light protection. God is light. God is love. God's light is your protection.

"Breathing slowly ... deeply. (Pause.) On the count of three, you will open your eyes, feeling very ... very good. One. Your breathing is getting deeper ... stronger. Feeling very, very good. Two. Slowly take a deep breath. Coming back. (Pause.) Feeling very, very good. Three." *End of meditation.

Group Discussion Checklist
   Did you breathe in the white light?
   Did you sense or see the white light enter your body?
   What, if anything, did you feel, sense, or see?
   Do you now feel more relaxed?
   What information do you have to offer about the meditation?
   Practice "Meditation to Create God Light Protection" on your own or with the group.

Third Eye
   The third eye is a psychic center located behind the bridge of the nose between the eyebrows. It is thought to be connected with the pineal and pituitary glands, which are located behind the center of the forehead in the interior of the brain. It is an energy point from which energy flows into and out of the body. In order to use the third eye to see images, it's necessary to close the eyes and quiet down the body. When

in meditation with the eyes closed, images or symbols may appear. This is known as "seeing with the third eye." A clairvoyant is a person who sees images and symbols within the mind's eye. A clairsentient is a person who senses a situation but does not actually see it. A clairaudent is a person who hears or senses a message in the head. All three psychic abilities are related to the third eye.

When meditating for the first time, a beginner may experience a slight pressure on the center of the forehead. This is a normal occurrence when the third eye is opening for the first time. This slight pressure may be felt several times until the third eye has adjusted to its new awareness. This is similar to flexing a muscle. If a muscle is flexed properly and often, that muscle will increase in strength. So too, does the third eye increase in its awareness when used often. When the third eye is open, a person is able to sense or see images from within. Thereafter, the third eye will open upon command without further prompting.

Group Discussion Checklist
Are you Clairvoyant: Do you see images within the mind's eye?
Are you Clairsentient? Do you sense but not see?
Are you Clairaudient? Do you hear or understand the message?
Are you all three?
With eyes closed, do you see dark, blurred images, or are the images white and clear? Explain.
Did you feel a slight pressure on the forehead when concentrating on the third eye?

Personal Guides
Personal guides are souls who have elected or have been chosen to guide you in this lifetime. Everyone has one or more personal guides. They are not here to serve you. They are here to guide you. Guides protect and influence humans on a day-to-day basis. They are the spiritual guidance that interacts with the conscious mind. Personal guides may act as your inner conscience, an intuition that warns you of danger or of making a mistake. They may encourage your decision by thought projection. They, along with your angels, may orchestrate synchronicity, allowing you to be in the right place at the right time for your spiritual advancement. We are all one with God. Therefore, angels,

personal guides, and guides are an extension of God and, at the same time, an extension of your higher self. The purpose of each meditation and exercise is to enhance your ability to see and sense your spiritual guidance.

Angels

Angels are a source of comfort, protection, and guidance. When you were born, it is believed you were assigned one or more angels to be with you daily. They are always nearby, but because of human limitations, most people are unable to see them.

Most humans can't see angels, even in the mind's eye, because angels vibrate at an extremely fast rate of speed. The faster the vibration, the more powerful and finer the essence. Imagine a fan rotating at a very fast rate of speed. The faster it spins, the less it is visible. This is similar to an angel's vibration. However, just because we can't see them doesn't mean they're not present. Angels are always available for our protection and guidance. Their compassion for all people is beyond human comprehension.

Each meditation will increase your ability to see or sense angels within the mind's eye. Angels may appear in different forms. They may be seen in the mind's eye as small white orbs, pale or bright circles of light, misty shadows, or transparent figures. An angel may appear with glowing wings fully expanded, as a glowing sphere of light, or as an ethereal mist. I have seen, in my mind's eye, clusters of angels as small as sparkles of light. They mentally communicated their name as *Ardents of Love*. I have seen angels taller than nine feet, while some appeared larger than a ten-story building. People who are spiritually aware may actually see the glowing light of angels with the physical eye. Usually, with the glow of the angel's light comes a message of comfort. An angel is recognized by the brilliant corona of light that radiates from its image, along with a feeling of peace and compassion. When an angel hovers near, its spiritual essence may blend into a person's energy, increasing the luminous glow of that person's aura.

Group Discussion Checklist

Have you seen an angel or guide in your mind's eye?

Have you felt or sensed an angel's or guide's presence? If so, share your experience.

Was there an occasion when you sensed or believed an angel had protected you from danger? If so, explain.

Do you sense when you are being guided or directed? If so, how?

Do you listen to your spiritual guides?

Have you ever regretted not listening to your intuition?

Suggest a book you have read about angels and guides.

Archangels

Archangels, angels, personal guides, and guides are on different levels or dimensions of spiritual progression, each having different roles. Archangels and angels are protectors. They also inspire and guide people on all spiritual matters. They are light beings. You are similar, inasmuch as you also are a light being, except you exist in a physical dimension while they exist in a spiritual dimension.

As stated in *The Secret Teaching of All Ages* by Manly P. Hall (paraphrase), "Archangels are said to be celestial bodies of light energy with four streamers or coronas of light with which the angels propel themselves through the subtle essence of their worlds. These streamers may appear as wings, but are actually brilliant bursts of spiritual light emanating from the archangels. When an archangel raises its arms, the burst of light is so intense that it appears, to the physical eye, as huge wings."

This is not a book about the different phylum of angels. There are far too many to mention. Rather, this book prepares the teacher and the novice to communicate with, and to sense an angel's guidance. Additional information on archangels, angels, personal guides, and guides will be presented as it applies to a specific exercise. Please take time for a thorough discussion of each checklist. Your personal experiences and your point of view can be very informative to the rest of the group. Discussions are extremely valuable. The variety of information offered by each person will broaden the group's awareness of spiritual guidance.

Group Discussion Checklist

Do you believe you have personal guides and/or angels? Explain.

Have you had a spiritual encounter? If so, explain.

Have you seen or sensed your angels or guides?

Have you had a physical encounter with an angel?

Have you physically felt an angel's touch? Explain.

What books on angels do you recommend? Why?

Brain-Wave Activity

The Greek letters beta, alpha, theta, and delta are used to describe various levels of brain-wave activity. Brain waves are measured in cycles per second (cps). High brain waves register when a person is awake; low brain waves in deep sleep. The pyramid indicates beta as the 10 percent of mental awareness humans commonly use in everyday life. During group meditation, the brainwave activity slows slows down, allowing the group's awareness to expand to alpha.

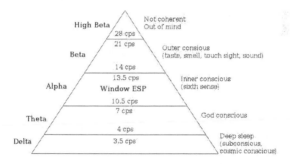

High beta is fast brain-wave activity. It is measured on an electroencephalograph (EEG) of 28 to 21 cps of brain-wave activity. High beta occurs when the brain waves speed up above the normal beta level. When a person becomes extremely angry or violent, the brain-wave cycles speed up, and the person may not be in full control of his or her thoughts or actions. People using drugs can reach an extremely high brain-wave activity, wherein reality is distorted and it's difficult to think clearly or rationally. They are easily fooled to believe their minds are expanding psychically, but in fact, they are not in full control of their minds at that time. People who are out of control may see images in their mind's eyes. They may believe they are having an insight into the spiritual realm. But in truth, they are visualizing a hallucination, an out-of-control perception. Influence of drugs is often referred to as a psychotic state of mind, a person who is not in his or her right mind.

Beta is the most common state of conscious action. Beta is measured on an EEG of 14 to 13.5 cps of brain-wave activity. Beta is the conscious level that maintains an awareness of the five senses—taste, smell, touch, sight, and sound. The human body uses the five senses as a means of receiving information. The conscious mind reasons information with logic, and the body reacts to the mind's directive. Commonly, most people have full use of the conscious mind but not the subconscious or super-subconscious mind. With practice, you can learn to slow down your brain waves and become aware of information in your subconscious and/or super-subconscious while still maintaining a conscious state of mind. This means you can remain deep in meditation and still be aware of everything happening around you.

Alpha is a deeper consciousness that can be reached through meditation. Extrasensory perception (ESP) is reached by slowing the brain-wave activity from 10.5 to 7 cycles per second. While in alpha, the window is open to numerous psychic abilities. At this level, you can sense more acutely and see psychically. Alpha level is sometimes signaled by a fluttering of the closed eyelids or rapid eye movement (REM).

During meditation, the brain produces the hormone serotonin. This is a natural, healthy secretion that produces a feeling of calm and happiness. Serotonin lessens fear and anxiety. While deep in meditation, don't hesitate to completely relax. The worst that can happen is the brain waves may slow down to delta as in deep sleep. If you do fall asleep, this is usually because your body needs the rest. The time spent in delta is energizing, and any sleep attained while in meditation will be beneficial to your physical body as well as the mental state of mind.

Theta is reached by a deeper meditation. Theta is measured on an EEG of 4 to 3.5 cps of brain-wave activity. It is a level of awareness where you can receive spiritual knowledge from the cosmic consciousness. While in theta, your soul may travel on the astral plane, interact with other dimensions, experience the existence of in-between life, or examine the true meaning of life. However, because this is a very deep level of awareness, most people don't remember those experiences. It's difficult to maintain theta and still be consciously aware. However, those who have mastered the control of very deep mediation may have the ability to remain consciously aware while in the state of theta.

Delta is the brain-wave level at which you dream. Most people dream about seven times a night, but most don't remember their dreams. While in a dream state, the subconscious mind will review its daily experiences. It may sort and reorganize its experiences and then file them into the subconscious mind to be reviewed and/or released at a later time. Sometimes in this dream state, the dreamer may receive messages from a deceased loved one. The message may remind the dreamer to become aware of a particular situation or to resolve a specific problem. If the dreamer remembers the dream, he or she should act upon that information.

While in delta sleep, the ethereal and soul bodies may rise up out of the physical body. At that time, they may travel on the astral plane, interact with different dimensions, enter a school of spiritual learning, or visit relatives who have passed over. Sometimes the dreamer may visit those who still exist on the physical plane.

Any touch or noise may startle the sleeper, thus drawing the soul and ethereal bodies back into the physical body. Sometimes the dreamer returns from the state of delta too quickly. He/she may dream of falling and awake with a sudden jolt. This may occur if the dreamer returns from the dream state so abruptly that the soul and ethereal bodies slam into the physical body with great force. This does not hurt the dreamer, except to startle the physical body, sometimes causing heart palpitations.

By following the meditations and exercises in the order provided, you will teach your brain to remain alert enough to interact with the dream, analyze it, and remember details of the dream upon waking. When awake, your conscious mind will use the dream information to deal with daily situations.

Group Discussion Checklist

Have you ever awakened abruptly from a deep sleep?

Have you dreamed of falling and then suddenly woke up?

Have you dreamed of receiving messages from a loved one, alive or deceased?

Have you dreamed of visiting another dimension?

Do you remember important dreams?

Do you take your dreams seriously and act upon the information received?

The Physical, Ethereal, and Soul Bodies

There are three basic parts to the human body—the physical, the ethereal, and the soul body. There are actually multidimensional aspects to a person's spiritual essence; however, for the beginner, let us examine only the three basic parts of the body.

The **physical body** can be seen and touched. It relates to taste, touch, smell, sight, and sound. Any physical assault upon the body is felt on a physical level as pain or trauma. The body also responds emotionally to the conscious and subconscious minds. Any mental shock causes stress, which in turn depletes the physical body of energy. The lack of vitality lessens the body's ability to heal itself. The physical body ages; time depletes its vitality, and death occurs.

The **ethereal body** is a reflection of the physical body. It displays itself as an aura, a luminous glow around the physical body. The aura may appear bright or dull, changing hourly or daily. Its glow may increase or decrease, according to the thought or influence the physical body is currently experiencing. When the aura is evenly displayed around the head or shoulders, it indicates the physical body is well balanced. It may be a reflection of a positive thought or emotion. If the aura appears dark, gray, or dingy, this indicates the body is reacting to a negative emotion or ailment. Sometimes the aura emits shafts or bubbles of light or gray colors. This indicates a leakage of energy resulting from a physical injury to that part of the body. The ethereal body (aura) reveals an illness long before the physical body becomes aware of its condition.

The **soul body** is the whole of all that you are. The soul is not a small speck of light in the heart, nor can it be measured in size or shape. The soul is so minute that medical doctors can barely detect its weight. It has been seen by one of my students, a psychic healer, as a dot of light rising from the physical body at the moment of death. The soul has been measured by Dr. Duncan MacDougall of Haverhill Massachusetts in 1907 as being a half ounce, more or less.

All people are born into the earth plane with a soul aura of transparent, pale, unchanging colors. These colors extend beyond the physical and ethereal bodies. The combination of colors represents the soul's higher self. Because the soul's essence is a very fine vibration, even most psychics rarely see the soul aura with the human eye. Yet, the soul is so immense and powerful that its essence can affect another person close by. As an example, the soul of Jesus has so much compassion and unconditional love that its essence can still be felt two thousand years after His physical death.

The **silver cord** is a string-like vibration or current that connects the soul and ethereal bodies to the physical body. It is the spiritual channel that conveys information to all three bodies. It is known as the lifeline to the physical body.

When asleep, the soul and ethereal bodies rise up away from the physical body. The silver cord remains attached and can stretch to infinity while the soul and ethereal bodies travel on the astral plane. The two bodies may investigate the spirit world or study with the masters on the astral plane. While the physical body is asleep, it is revitalizing its energy and health. If the physical body is startled, the silver cord snaps the soul and the ethereal bodies back into the physical body abruptly. Many people have experienced this as a jolt awakening them out of a deep sleep. At the end of one's life, usually when the physical body is depleted of life's vitality, the soul and ethereal bodies make their final separation from the physical body. The silver cord disconnects, and physical existence ceases to be. The soul and ethereal essences cross over into the next dimension.

To create a visual analogy, imagine the physical body as an old, worn-out shoe. The shoe has served its purpose. The spiritual bodies don't need the old shoe anymore, so the silver cord releases, and the soul and ethereal bodies rise out of the physical body. They look down at the old shoe. They have no concern about the condition of the shoe. They may, or may not, realize they had once worn the shoe. Their feelings are usually, but not always, detached and emotionless. They don't judge the condition of the shoe, nor how it came to be the way it is. The soul is undiscriminating. The soul and ethereal bodies rise up out of the physical body toward the God light. The worn-out shoe (the physical body) will be tended to by those family members who are left behind.

Group Discussion Checklist

Have you traveled the astral plane in a dream state? Explain.

Have you ever felt you were outside your body? Explain.

Have you seen the silver cord release from a dying body?

Share your knowledge of the three parts of the body.

Are your dreams mental communication rather than astral traveling?

Explain how *you* define the difference. As each person grows more spiritual, his or her new awareness will change the definition of astral travel and dream communication.

Chapter 2
THE BLACK BOX

The Black Box is a random exercise that begins when two or three members arrive. One person will put an object in a black box and then place the box in the center of the room. As each member arrives, he/she will mentally tune into the black box and attempt to visualize what is inside. The Black Box exercise is a good way to liven up the group and encourage the members to socialize. Searching the mind's eye to discover the box's contents is another way to strengthen the mind's eye and increase psychic awareness.

Preparation of a Black Box

A shoe box, candy box, or any medium- to small-sized box may be used. The outside of the box should be painted black to cover any print, designs, or price tags. Any writing or design remaining on the box might alter the vibrations and influence one's impression of the box's contents.

Contents

A piece of jewelry, icon, or any small object is placed inside the box. It's best to begin with a metal object. Metal holds stronger vibrations than cloth or paper does. Therefore, it's easier for a beginner to sense its vibrations. A small metal broach in the shape of a star, flower, or animal may be placed in the box. Each object will carry a vibration relating to its design or to the owner of the jewelry. A religious article, such as a cross, holy picture, or printed prayer card, will carry a religious feeling.

A photograph of a person may contain the person's personality or daily activities. A handwritten signature may hold the signer's personality or emotions on the day the signature was signed. A photograph of a bride and groom might carry strong vibrations of the wedding celebration or of the person's emotions on that day. A baby's toy might resonant with the infant's feelings or the mother's love for the baby. An aromatic herb placed in the black box could transmit an aroma, even though the fragrance is not strong enough to be physically smelled. A brightly colored object, such as a crayon or piece of cloth, may be placed inside the box. Some members might find it easier to see or sense color than to read the emotions of an object.

The object could be an antique. An old ring could communicate many different vibrations belonging to the era in which it was once worn or the previous owner. Because it once belonged to someone who had a lifetime of experiences, the ring would surely resonant with many different vibrations.

Exercise 1. The Black Box

The members may approach the box, wander around it, or sit randomly near the box. However, it would be more psychically effective to sit in a circle. A circle will retain the group's energy. The members will take a long, deep breath, hold it as long as is comfortable, and then slowly exhale until they have reached their own levels of awareness. As the physical body calms down, the mind becomes acutely aware. It is at this deeper level of awareness that vibrations within the box can be seen or sensed in the mind's eye.

The eyes may be open or closed. If the eyes remain open, it's recommended to close the eyes from time to time. Vibrations can be seen within the mind's eye more easily than with the physical eye. Focus on the box. Mentally tune into the particles of energy surrounding the object. The energy will hold memories of past or current events in which that object was (or is currently) involved. Don't touch or shake the box. Don't lift the box to feel the weight or listen to the sound of the object as it is jostled about. The hands may be placed over or near the box to feel the vibrations emanating from the box. This is a mental communication between the person and the box's contents.

Some members may choose to walk around the box or hover over it. Some may prefer to concentrate on the box at close range. The eyes may be open or closed as the members place their hands near the object. Vibrations may be seen in the mind's eye as shapes, forms, symbols, or images. They may appear clear, blurred, or fragmented. The reader will analyze an image or symbol as it relates to his or her own experience.

Some may choose to remain in their seats, close their eyes, and use their imaginary hands to reach into the box. The ethereal hands are an extension of the physical hands. They can psychically touch, feel, sense, or move the object. Mentally imagine the ethereal hands touching the object. People who are clairsentient will have a keener sense of feeling. They feel emotion rather than see symbols or pictures in their mind's eye.

Some members may choose to analyze the box at a distance. It wouldn't make any difference if the box had been in the center of the room or in another building. Neither time nor distance can obstruct mental communication. However, vibrations can be altered by negative thoughts. It's not the vibrations that are altered. It's the person's inability to reach beyond the negative vibration.

A positive attitude will make it easier connect with the vibrations. To sense a vibration, you must slow down your brain waves and direct your attention toward the object without hesitancy of failure. Don't say, "I don't think I can do this." This sends out negative vibrations and can neutralize the positive energy, interfering with your ability to see within the mind's eye. Any negative thought can create a barrier, alter the impression you are receiving, and cause the information to become faulty. Negative energy is created by fear or disbelief in one's self. Positive energy is a strong, concentrated energy that can be used as a means of communication much like radio waves.

Some members may place a piece of paper on his or her lap and allow the hand to draw the shape or design. Hold the pencil upright so the hand is not touching the paper. To begin writing, move the hand in a circular motion several times and then let the hand do the work. Allow the hand to flow freely.

Perhaps you have acquired the ability to receive information from your personal guides. If so, don't hesitate to ask for assistance, even if it's only for practice. Any communication to and from your guides will increase your spiritual connection. At the end of each exercise, be sure to mentally thank your guides for their assistance and bless them for coming, even if you had not been aware of their presence. Perhaps there had been more spiritual contact than you realize. Because we are human in form, we cannot fully comprehend the complexity of the many spiritual sources that are present to assist us.

The group may discuss the box's contents before the beginning or at the end of each session. Each person will give his or her impression of what had been seen, sensed, or drawn on paper. The group may discuss the emotions connected to the object or what images came to mind. Don't worry if your images or symbols seem weird, strange, or unexplainable. It's quite common to see comical or indescribable symbols. This will occur until each person has clarified the meaning of his or her own symbols.

After each member has told what they believe is in the box, the box is opened. Now the group can discuss with more clarity what their own symbols could have meant. Each time this exercise is repeated and a discussion follows, it will bring a clearer understanding of symbols. A symbol may have an entirely different meaning to one person as to another. People relate to a symbol through their own experiences. It's each member's responsibility to analyze and learn his or her own symbols.

Example:

Today, the box would contain a school graduation ring. After reading the vibrations, one person might say, "I see a cap and gown. I think it belongs to someone who just graduated." The cap and gown is considered a hit because it relates to graduation. One person may sense a hard, circular shape. The circular shape, representing the ring, is considered a hit. A person might feel or sense the object is hard, silver, or small. That's also a hit. One might see a spiraling effect but not understand the spiraling symbol had referred to the round shape of the ring. Some may sense a size, shape, or color but are unable to put a name to it. A person might call out the name of the ring without hesitation. Or a person might draw a round shape. They may logically think it's a shiny ball. However, even though they had drawn the correct shape, their logic may have taken over, and they had guessed at the contents.

To determine the box's content:

- Sense the size and shape.
- What color do you see? Is it hard or soft?
- Is there an emotion attached to the object? Does it feel happy or sad?
- Does it feel warm or cold?
- What symbols come to mind?
- Does the symbol remind you of a holiday, event, or person?
- Visualize your ethereal hands inside the box.
- Project your mind into the center of the box.
- Mentally ask your guide(s) to assist.

Begin reading the contents inside the black box.

Group Discussion Checklist

What, if any, symbols did you see?
Did you correctly analyze a symbol?
Was a color easier to sense than a shape or an emotion?
Were you able to visualize any part of the object?
Did you sense the object, not see it?
Were you able to feel with your ethereal hands?
Did you draw the object?
Did you sense your guides assisting?
Did you thank your guides for assisting?

Chapter 3
MEDITATION, VISUALIZATION, AND AURA READING

The following meditations are presented in a specific order to relax the physical body, visualize images within the third eye, slow down the brain waves at will, and at the same time remain in full control of the mind and body while in meditation. As preparation to future teaching, each member is encouraged to take turns reading several paragraphs aloud.

Preparation to Meditation

Dim the lights. A dimly lit room makes it easier to see within the mind's eye. The phone should be taken off the hook, and cell phones turned off. Do not smoke or drink alcohol before meditating. A clear state of mind is necessary to achieve a deep level of meditation. Avoid eating a heavy meal before meditation. The mind will focus more clearly if it's not distracted by the stomach processing food.

Recreational drugs should never be used. It's best to wear loose-fitting clothing. Nothing tight should be worn around the waist, as this will restrict deep breathing. The shoes may be removed to allow the auric energy to easily anchor to the earth's energy. Sit erect so the spine is straight and the head is upright. Do not cross the legs at the knees as this will twist the spine and obstruct the flow of energy up the spine. The legs may be crossed at the ankles, as this does not obstruct the flow of energy. Don't cross the arms over the chest. This is a negative symbol of blocking with rebellion. Blocking sets up a negative energy field, obstructing sensitivity.

It's important to begin all meditations by relaxing the top of the head first and then proceeding down the body, ending at the toes. When starting at the head, the mind becomes acutely alert and intuitively awake, and it is more capable of mentally controlling all parts of the body.

Prayer

The group may mentally pray or recite a prayer of protection before meditating. Any prayer may be used if it's prayed with sincerity. The words may change daily if a member intuitively senses a different need. There are many ways to pray, but the purpose should conform to the current need or request. The best prayer is one that comes from the heart with a complete understanding of its purpose. Dim the lights. Sit up straight. Close your eyes. One person may recite the prayer, or the group may mentally say their own personal prayer. The following prayer is only a suggestion.

Prayer of Protection

"We call upon the God light. We ask our angels and guides to stand by for protection, guidance, and direction. We thank God for the highest spiritual guidance we are capable of using."

Meditation to Awaken the Third Eye is intentionally a short meditation. It is intended to stimulate the mind's eye, strengthen psychic awareness, and set up a force field of white-light protection. Each meditation produces the hormone serotonin, a neurotransmitter that increases mental awareness, relaxes the body, and lessens fear and anxiety. The following meditation will be used many times in different exercises. If meditating as a single person or in a group, the following meditations may be prerecorded.

Meditation to Awaken the Third Eye

"Slowly take a deep breath and hold it as long as is comfortable. As you slowly exhale, feel the relaxation going down your face. You're breathing slowly … deeply. (Pause.) Your jaw is relaxing. Your face is relaxing. Slowly take a deep breath, and hold it as long as is comfortable. As you exhale, relax your forehead.

"Your eyes are relaxing ... relaxing ... relaxing. Concentrate on your forehead. Within your mind's eye you see a small white light. Visualize the light growing brighter ... brighter ... brighter. (Pause.) The light is softening. It's becoming larger ... and larger until it forms a cloud of white light. Breathing in the God light. (Pause.) God is light. God is love. Visualize the light growing brighter ... and brighter. Filling the room with God's light ... and God's love. This is your God light protection. (Pause.) On the count of three, you will open your eyes feeling very, very good. (Pause.) Coming back. One. Your breathing is getting deeper ... and stronger. Two. You're feeling very, very good. Three. Open your eyes."

*End of meditation.

Group Discussion Checklist
    Did you feel relaxed and calm during meditation?
    Did you feel a pressure as the third eye opened?
    Is your third eye already open?
    Did you visualize or create the white light?
    Did you see or sense the white light without trying?
    What, if anything, did you see or sense?
    Practice Meditation to Awaken the Third Eye often to strengthen psychic awareness.

The following Body Relaxation Meditation is designed to lower the brainwaves though controlled breathing. With practice, you will be able to use your mind and your breathing to relax your body at will, remain in a state of relaxation while at work, alone, or in a crowd, and enjoy a deep, restful night's sleep. Practice this simple meditation until a peaceful state of mind becomes a natural part of your being.

Body Relaxation Meditation

"Slowly take a deep breath and hold it as long as is comfortable. As you slowly exhale, feel the calmness flowing through your body. Releasing all your cares ... all your problems. You're breathing slowly ... deeply. Breathing in. (Pause.) Imagine the God light wrapping around your body. God is light. God is love.

"You're breathing slowly, deeply. Your body is relaxing … relaxing. (Pause.) Slowly take a deep breath and hold it as long as is comfortable. As you exhale, your face is relaxing. (Pause.) Your eyes are relaxing. (Pause.) You're breathing slowly … deeply. Your forehead is relaxing. (Pause.) Your jaw is relaxing. Slowly take a deep breath and hold it as long as is comfortable. As you exhale, your chest relaxing. Your stomach is relaxing. (Pause.)

"Feel the relaxation going down your back. Your spine is relaxing. You're breathing slowly, deeply. Your arms are relaxing. Your fingers are relaxing. Slowly take a deep breath and hold it as long as is comfortable. (Pause.) As you exhale, feel the relaxation going down your legs. Your feet are relaxing. You're feeling very … very peaceful. Breathing slowly … deeply. (Pause for several minutes or as long as agreed upon.)

"You are now coming back. On the count of three, you will open your eyes. (Pause.) One. Your breathing is getting deeper … stronger. Feeling very, very good. Two. Your breathing is getting deeper … stronger. Three. Your eyes are open, and you're feeling very, very good."

*End of meditation.

You have now learned to relax your body through controlled breathing. When daily chores seem too hectic and you need to quiet down, remember the easy method of deep breathing. Take one long, deep breath and then exhale slowly. This will usually relax the body. Most people take small, shallow breaths. Practice deep breathing daily. This will stretch the lungs so they will become more pliable, healthier. Each deep breath will bring additional oxygen to the brain. Oxygen is needed for clear thinking and mental concentration. This simple breathing method will release tension from the facial muscles; it will allow the veins to circulate blood more freely and bring oxygen and nourishment to the face and body. Relaxing the facial muscles will also help prevent wrinkles or new frown lines from forming. Each time the group meets, a different member should recite the meditation as preparation for future teaching. Eventually, the group may choose the speaker best suited to recite the meditation.

Group Discussion Checklist
    Has your ability to see the God light increased?
    Did you feel your facial muscles relax?

Did you feel parts of your body relax upon command?

What other values do you attribute to this meditation?

How did you feel while meditating?

Can you now relax your face at will, with your eyes open or closed?

Use the deep breathing method often to relax your body at will with your eyes open.

How to See an Aura

An **aura** is a luminous essence surrounding the human body. Energy circulates through the body and gives off an auric glow similar to a halo. This glow is an essence of the ethereal body. In our limited, three-dimensional world, light waves that are above or below a certain vibrational range are not visible to the human eye. But that doesn't mean they're not there. The aura is present whether we see it or not. The human eyes can only pick up a certain range of light, but when these waves or vibrations have enough intensity, those who are sensitive or psychic are able to perceive them as auras of light surrounding the human body. There are two parts to an aura.

The **inner aura**, which is closest to the body, is a reflection of the ethereal body. Its white glow extends one to five inches beyond the physical body and is usually seen around the head and shoulders. The extent and brightness of the aura varies from person to person and from day to day. The mind and body are structurally and functionally a single unit. A person thinks not with the brain but through the brain. Each thought or emotion emits a different wavelength and degree of aura light. The aura displays the present state of health, mental, and emotional attitude of a person on any given day.

When the mind and body are in peaceful harmony, the inner aura is usually bright and luminous, and it may extend several inches beyond the physical body. However, if the mind or body are in disharmony with its thoughts or surroundings or have experienced an emotional trauma or negative experience, the aura may appear dull, pale, or nonexistent. Any physical illness or mental disharmony depletes the physical body of energy and, in turn, depletes the auric glow. If the body experiences a disease or an injury, a portion of the aura may rise as a bubble or spew out rays or flashes of light or gray color at the point of distress. Any damage to the physical body creates a change in the aura. A psychic can sense or see an internal injury rising from the aura, even if the injury is not yet visible to the naked eye.

The **outer aura** is also an essence of the ethereal body. It consists of fluctuating colors that may extend several inches beyond the white inner aura. Each color represents a vibratory display of personality or character. The colors of the outer aura change with each thought, emotion, or feeling, manifesting a combination of vibratory colors belonging to that thought, emotion, or feeling. Each hue or tint, whether it is intensely brilliant or dull and dingy, exhibits a specific degree of energy created by the thought or emotion of that person at that moment in time. The colors of the aura reveal the emotional makeup of the person and the positive or negative forces acting upon the body at the time.

People who are spiritually aware or are in communion with spiritual beings or angels may radiate an outer aura of pink blending to pale orchid. Because the outer aura is a finer, more subtle energy, it is seldom seen by most people.

The **soul aura** extends beyond the outer aura. It is the whole of who you are. Because it's an extremely subtle vibratory energy, it's not usually seen by normal sight. The soul aura has been seen on photographs displaying one main color, usually but not always shades of blue blended with the outer aura colors. The inner and outer auras may change from hour to hour or day to day, but the soul aura remains the same color as the day of birth. Even though the ethereal body may occasionally display a gray aura reflecting emotional or physical damage to the body, the soul aura does not change color. The soul is not harmed by a physical experience because it resides in perfect harmony with its own nature.

The holy aura has been painted on many canvases as a halo of light surrounding spiritual people dating back to early periods in time. Auras have been illustrated on different forms of art and carved on the walls of caves throughout the world. Auras have been seen on paintings by American-Indian, Hindu, and Persian art. You have no doubt seen a religious painting in which a luminous glow radiates from the body of a saintly figure, in particular the head of Christ, the Virgin Mary, or the apostles. The holy aura is usually shown as a white or golden halo around the head or as a glow surrounding the whole body.

Similar auras have been depicted on Buddhist holy men as light emanating from the crown chakra located at the top of the head or the eye chakra on the forehead. The aura surrounding the holiest was most likely painted because the artist had used his or her extrasensory perception (ESP) and had captured the true essence of his or her model. Even if the model (holy person) had been deceased a long time ago, the artist could still tune into that person's soul while painting the picture. If the artist maintained a meditative state of mind, he/she would be more likely to see the glow as it reflected the model's spirituality, even if the model was not present. A person who is not in a peaceful state of mind is less likely to see a holy aura. Consider the aura of Jesus Christ. His aura of love and compassion for humankind is still felt over thousands of years later. His spiritual aura still affects many people, even today.

Group Discussion Checklist
What have you experienced regarding an aura?
What pictures have you seen of holy auras?
On what figures or places have auras been depicted?

Sound of Color Vibrations
Do you know why your thoughts are important? Do you know what happens to each thought you send out into the atmosphere? As a thought occurs, it sends out a vibratory pattern of colors belonging to that thought. Each (thought) color vibrates at a specific frequency that can be heard and seen by angels and guides. Angels are in tune with all color and sound vibrations and have the ability to interpret their true meanings. Angels know your thoughts by the colors of the aura you are emitting. They are drawn to help as they see or hear the colors flowing from your aura. In fact, angels see your emotional stress long before you even think of calling out for help. The color, shade, or hue of your aura will bring an angel who is concerned with assisting you in that specific need, or in answer to a specific thought or prayer. No matter how subtle your thought is, an angel understands and is ready to help. You don't have to call for help; your thought has already summoned them.

While deep in meditation, I have seen, in my mind's eye, musical notes and vibrating waves of color. I intuitively understood this to be a communication in another dimension. Musical notes are sometimes seen in the mind's eye, flowing from the aura of a person in prayer. The symbol of musical notes is a way the human mind interprets the meaning. Humans analyze symbols as they relate to their own learned experiences.

Exchanging Energy

Your body discharges and exchanges aura energy daily. It radiates outward and can influence each person with whom you come in contract. When you stand close to a person, you may sense his or her aura as a feeling or an emotion. That person, in turn, may sense your aura in the same way. The closer you stand, the more intensely the auras can be felt or sensed. You have no doubt heard the expression concerning how she has "left an impression on me." When a person is sad, you may sense sadness, or when happy, you will feel happy. If the person's thoughts are intense, fragments of emotions may become attached to your aura, even after that person has left the room, and may cling for days or months. They have a lasting effect.

Group Discussion Checklist

Discuss how you can sense another person's emotion, even though you cannot see the aura.

Have you seen another person's attitude reflected in his or her aura?

Has someone's attitude affected you? If so, explain.

Has someone left an impression on you? Was it sorrow or joy?

What holy person has left an impression on you?

Group Viewing of an Aura

For this exercise, each person will take a turn standing at the front of the room to display his or her aura. The background should be a light-colored wall, or a white sheet may be hung as a backdrop. The aura is best seen at dusk or in a dimly lit room. Some viewers may prefer to sit on the floor. When the eyes are cast slightly upward, as if looking up at the top of a mountain, brain waves tend to slow down, making aura viewing easier. Don't look directly at the body. Look beyond it.

An aura is most commonly seen as a luminous glow slightly above the head and shoulders.

If the person displaying his or her aura is energetic or spiritually inclined that day, the aura may be seen easily with open eyes. If the aura is dull or nearly nonexistent, it may indicate that person has low energy or has negative thoughts. In that case, the viewer will concentrate within his or her forehead, the third eye, and observe the person's aura with closed eyes.

On the other hand, there will be days when the viewer will see clearly because he/she is healthy or spiritually in tune that day. A healthy person will find it easier to tune into the psychic energy of an aura. However, there will be times when the viewer is not feeling up to par and the ability to see the aura will be lessened that day. When an aura cannot be seen with open eyes, the viewer should try closing the eyes and looking within the mind's eye. Try both ways. See which way is best that day.

A false aura may appear as a white halo. If the viewer's eyes are strained or tired, his or her eyes may see a white glow instead of an aura. Though it may look like an aura, it may not be a true aura. To be sure you are seeing a true aura, blink your eyes or close your eyes from time to time. Rest them for several seconds and then resume gazing at the aura. Don't stare hard at the aura, as this will tire the eyes and create a white glow, which is a false illusion of an aura.

Group Discussion Checklist
Have you seen an aura? If so, explain.
Have you seen different colors in an aura? If so, explain.
Have you seen a negative person's aura? If so, explain.
Are you clairvoyant? Can you see an aura?
Are you clairsentient? Can you sense an aura?

Exercise 1. Viewing an Aura

One person will stand in front of the room to display his or her aura. The remaining members will remain seated. The members will slow down their brain waves by taking slow, deep breaths and then exhale slowly, allowing the body and mind to relax. The members will imagine a white light in the mind's eye. They will mentally draw the white light in through the top of their head and then through their body. They may rest their hands on the lap, palms up, and then mentally direct the light out through the hands toward the person standing at the front of the room. This additional energy sent by the group will be used by the person displaying his or her aura.

This exercise can be done by one person without the class present. The viewer will look in a mirror to see his or her own aura.

The person displaying an aura may use any of the following techniques:

- Intensify the brightness of the aura. Take a deep breath. Mentally force energy out the top of the head. This will increase the luminous glow or project a flare or bubble of light out the top of the head.
- Pray silently. A prayer sincerely said or thought has been known to create an aura of pale orchid or pink around the head and shoulders.
- Mentally communicate with an angel or guide. Ask it to stand next to or emerge within your aura. An angelic presence merged with the aura will generate a brighter aura. Sometimes a luminous image or a white ball of energy may be seen slightly above the head, indicating a guide or spirit is hovering nearby. An angelic presence will emit a feeling of serenity and celestial harmony, but a spirit's presence will not. Be sure to thank the angel or guide for its display of energy.
- After several months of practice viewing the aura, the group may have increased their psychic abilities enough to allow a past-life memory to present itself within the aura. The person may mentally suggest a past-life memory present itself in his or her aura. Past lives may manifest in several ways.

A past life may:

- A past-life memory can be seen as a translucent glow or as part of an image hovering beside, over, or in front of the person. Even though this glow may appear similar to an angel, the feeling of complete compassion that an angel exudes is not felt by the presence of a past-life memory.

- A past-life memory may appear as a haze or transparent form superimposed in front of the face. The haze may project an impression or an ethnic facial feature of that past life. This may be seen or sensed as a personality unlike the subject's present personality.
- A past life may not be seen but only sensed as a different personality.
- A past life may be sensed as a specific personality or as having lived in a different location of the world.
- Don't be disappointed if a past life doesn't present itself when first beginning aura reading. Past life projection takes time and practice.

Further discussions on how to project and read a past life will be discussed in chapter nine. Dim the lights and begin "Exercise 1. Viewing an Aura."

Group Discussion Checklist

Did you mentally force a brighter aura?

Did you see the aura with open or closed eyes?

Do you sense rather than see the aura? Are you clairsentient?

Do you see colors or glowing spheres? Are you clairvoyant?

What, if any, colors were most prominent?

Were the colors you saw confirmed by another person?

Did an aura reflect a current health condition?

Did you see or sense bubbles or flashes of light over an injured area?

Did you see or sense an angelic energy near or within an aura?

There is no right or wrong way to see an aura. Use the method that is most natural for you. Do it your way. Repeat this exercise often until aura viewing is successful.

Exercise 2. Viewing the Aura in a Mirror

This exercise does not require group participation. In a dimly lit room or at dusk, stand in front of a mirror. Recite a prayer of protection either aloud or mentally to yourself. Take a slow, deep breath. As you exhale, feel your brain waves slowing down. Continue gazing in the mirror. Again, take a slow, deep breath, breathing in the Godlike energy. With your mind, mentally force energy out the top of your head. A glow of luminous light may shoot out from the top of the head. Continue concentrating on the aura. Breathe in and then force the energy out your head and shoulders. This aura is usually white and may extend several inches past the physical body. As you increase your energy by deep breathing, concentrate on the aura growing brighter and larger.

Begin "Exercise 2. Viewing an Aura in a Mirror."

Group Discussion Checklist
  Did the aura grow brighter or larger upon breathing in the light?
  Did you see a flash of light shoot out from the top of the head?
  Were you able to force the glow of the aura out of the top of the head?
  Share your experience of viewing the aura in a mirror.

Exercise 3. Viewing a Spiritual Aura

Viewing a spiritual aura can be a group exercise or can be done in the privacy of your own home. To see your own spiritual aura, stand in front of a mirror and take a long, deep breath. Exhale slowly, allowing your brain waves to slow down. Mentally ask your guides or angels for "protection, guidance, and directions." Again, take a long, deep breath, calming the body. Continue slow, deep breathing. Mentally or aloud, recite a prayer or think a spiritual thought. A sincere prayer or spiritual thought will change the color of the aura. Prayer usually emits a delicate pale pink and/or a soft orchid glow around the head if the prayer is recited with sincerity. Don't come to the mirror with an attitude that you are going to prove that you can create a spiritual aura. There must be a sincere desire, not a demand for proof. Be sure to thank your guides and angels for their assistance.

Begin "Exercise 3 Viewing a Spiritual Aura."

Group Discussion Checklist
  Did you mentally or verbally recite a prayer of protection? If so, what prayer did you use?
  Did you produce a spiritual aura? If so, what colors appeared?
  Did you remember to thank your guides or angels?

Did you attempt to see your own aura with closed eyes?

Exercise 4. Feeling an Aura

The members will place their chairs in as perfect a circle as possible. The energy created by the members and their spirit guides will surround the circle with protection. A wooden stool is placed in the center of the circle. Avoid using a metal chair, as the metal could interfere with the vibrations or currents of energy. Select one member to sit in the center of the circle. This person is known as the sitter. One or two members will then attempt to read the sitter's aura by touch. They are known as the readers. The remaining members will place their hands on their lap, draw white-light energy in through the top of their heads, and send it out through their hands to the readers.

The readers may do any of the following:

- The readers will move their hands slowly around the sitter's body, never touching the physical body, only the auric field.
- A smooth aura may indicate the sitter is peaceful. It may project a calming effect upon the reader.
- An irritated sitter may emit an irregular or spastic energy. The reader may sense or feel an irritation.
- If the sitter carries many small problems, the reader will sense a need to brush his or her hands across the sitter's shoulders, brushing away the problems.
- The reader may feel an unusual flare of energy near an injury.
- The reader's hand may intuitively stop at the injured area. A cold, hot, or warm area may signal a distressed area.
- An injury can be sensed or felt as a bump or flare in the aura.
- The reader's hand may tingle, signaling a healing is needed. The reader will then draw in the God light through the top of the head and then send it out the fingertips to the sitter.
- The reader may feel a drag or a pull on the hand as it passes over an injured area. This is because the injured area lacks positive energy.
- If the sitter has an injury or an internal ailment, he/she should not tell the readers where or what the injury is. The readers

will try to detect the injury by touching, feeling, or sensing the sitter's aura.

- A person who is physically healthy and has a high-energy field may emit an aura several inches to several feet out from the physical body. The reader may not need to come very close in order to feel a large aura.

Each person may have his or her own unique way of detecting an injury or illness. Use your natural instinct to sense or see an aura.

Begin "Exercise 4. Feeling an Aura."

Group Discussion Checklist

Did you feel or sense a difference in each person's aura?

Did the aura feel peaceful, calm, or smooth?

Did you locate an injury? If so, how?

Did you locate any bumps or flares in the aura?

Did the aura vibrate or feel irritated? Explain.

Which sitter was peaceful, as opposed to another who was anxious?

Did you attempt to see or sense the aura with closed eyes?

What, if anything, did you see or sense within the mind's eye?

Did you experience a powerful aura, one that projected several feet out from the sitter's body?

How far away from the sitter's body did you feel the aura? What information did this aura tell you?

Did you direct the healing of God light toward a sitter?

Aura Colors

The following aura colors are the most commonly accepted ones. The class need not go through the complete list, but a group discussion of several colors will help the group understand their meanings.

Purple: Spiritual. Spiritual wisdom.

Clear Violet: Highly spiritual. Royal color. Rarely seen in a typical aura. Rays of power and influence. People who are tolerant in love and wisdom radiate hues of violet.

Violet Shading to Blue: Signs of transcending idealism.

Amethyst: Power, grandeur, and accomplishment. Amethyst is spiritual.

Blue: Spiritual progression. Truth. Inspiration. Often associated with the feminine aspect of the divine (i.e., Virgin Mary).

Indigo or dark blue: Spiritual qualities. Integrity, sincerity. Dark blue is often seen as a narrow ribbon bordering the outer edge of an aura which indicates a spiritual nature.

Yellow shading to gold: Spiritual wisdom.

Green: Strength, progress, and regeneration. Combination of yellow (wisdom) and pure blue (truth).

Pure green: Vitality and energy, both spiritual and physical. Healer. Shades of green should be displayed in the home. Its vibrations are extremely refreshing to the soul.

Deep or dark green: Individual growth. Achieved prosperity (i.e., money).

Olive green: Deceit and treachery.

Dark green: Negative aspects of envy and jealousy.

Yellow: Wisdom or spiritual wisdom. Thought and mental concentration.

Yellow rays: Optimistic. Power to dispel fear and worry.

Gold: Spiritual.

Yellow shading to gold: A soul developing spiritual qualities.

Orange: Vitality. Combination of red (vitality) and yellow (wisdom). Health and wisdom if the color is pure. Used by spiritual healers. Well balanced. Excellent mixers.

Pink: Refined quality. Mysticism present. Awakening to self-realization and spiritual awareness.

Red: Denotes life, strength, affection, and vitality. Strong mind and will. Materialistic.

Bright, clear red: Generous, praiseworthy, ambitious.

Crimson: Sensuality.

Deep scarlet: Lust.

Muddy red: Negative influence. Can be selfish. Display of anger.

Brown: Industrious. An organizer. Lacking emotion. Conventional, persevering. Businessman's color. Don't expect strong emotional feelings or tendencies in brown-tinged auras.

Light brown: Desire of industrial or material growth.

Silver: Inconsistent. Changeable moods. Lively but unreliable personality. Usually jack-of-all-trades, master of none. Gifted in matter of movement, speech, and travel.

Gray: Loner. Lack of imagination. Negative thoughts.

Black: Corrupt or negative thoughts. Spiteful, sinister. Negation of good.

Group Discussion Checklist

What aura colors have you seen?

What aura colors give a hint of peacefulness?

What aura colors give a warning of negativity?

Preparation to 8-8 Method of Breathing

If you have trouble concentrating while down in meditation, then Meditation to 8-8 Method of Breathing should solve that problem. The following meditation is designed to hold your mind focused as your brain waves slow down to alpha level. The method of counting while deep breathing holds the mind's attention on each number, thus preventing the mind from wandering onto trivial matters of the day.

During this meditation, you will be asked to breathe in to the count of eight. Hold your breath to the count of four. Then release your breath to the count of eight. If you're unable to hold the breath to the count of eight, then ignore the numbers and count to your own rhythm. With each slow, deep breath, you will feel the chest rise, filling the lungs with air, more air than you would usually inhale. The deeper the breath, the more oxygen is filtered into the lungs. Oxygen is then dispersed through the cells, organs, and the entire body. The mind will react more quickly with a good circulation of oxygen. Deep breathing will encourage the lungs to be used to their fullest capacity. Shallow breathing does not allow the lung to stretch or expand in a healthy manner.

During meditation, you will slow down the brain waves so the right side of the brain—the intuitive brain—becomes more active. This will increase your ability to visualize within the mind's eye. You will repeatedly hear the phrases "going deeper and deeper." Each time you hear the words "deeper and deeper," you will concentrate on your forehead—the mind's eye. You will also be asked several times to "become pure mind." These phrases will encourage full concentration by the mind. Usually, you will not be aware of any part of the body, except the mind. During the meditation, you will also be reminded by the phrases "knowing exactly where you are at all times" and "knowing exactly what you're doing." Repetition of these phrases reinforces the mind to maintain both conscious and subconscious awareness at the same time.

Meditation to 8-8 Method of Breathing

"Close your eyes. Visualize a cloud of white light surrounding your body. God is light. God is love. (Pause.) This is your God light protection. Slowly take a deep breath and hold it as long as is comfortable. As you exhale, release all your cares ... all your problems. Your face is relaxing. (Pause.) Breathing very slowly ... very deeply. Going deeper ... and deeper ... into awareness. Becoming pure mind. (Pause.) Knowing exactly where you are at all times. Knowing exactly what you're doing.

"Slowly take a deep breath and hold it as long as is comfortable. You are relaxing ... relaxing ... relaxing. Breathe in, two, three, four, five, six, seven, eight. Hold (your breath), two, three, four. Out (exhale), two, three, four, five, six, seven, eight. (Repeat three times or more if necessary.)

"You are now feeling very, very relaxed. Concentrate on your mind's eye. Visualize a white light. (Pause.) The light is becoming larger ... brighter. Sense the love within the light. (Pause.) Breathing very slowly. Very deeply. Your body is relaxing. Going deeper ... and deeper into awareness. Knowing exactly where you are at all times. Knowing exactly what you're doing. *You* are in control. Going deeper ... and deeper into a new awareness. Becoming pure mind.

"Concentrate on the mind's eye. Beautiful white images are drifting toward you. Communicate. Enjoy. Listen to the message. (Pause several minutes or as long as agreed upon.) Mentally bless the images. Thank them for coming. Breathing very slowly ... very deeply. You are now coming back. On the count of three, you will open your eyes. One. Your breathing is getting deeper ... stronger. Two. Feeling very good. Three. Open your eyes."

*End of meditation.

Use the 8-8 Method of Breathing often until it becomes natural to take slow, deep breaths. Deep breathing should become a daily habit, whether in meditation or during everyday activities. The Meditation to 8-8 Method of Breathing and the Body Relaxation Meditation are different techniques to strengthen and hold one's attention while down in meditation. They may be used separately or combined as follows:

Meditation to 8-8 Method of Breathing and Meditation to Relax the Body

"Slowly take a deep breath and hold it as long as is comfortable. As you exhale, release all your cares … all your problems. Breathing very slowly … very deeply. Feeling very relaxed, very peaceful. (Pause.) Going deeper … and deeper into awareness. Becoming pure mind. Imagine a light wrapping around you. God is light. God is love. Your body is relaxing … relaxing. (Pause.)

"Slowly take a deep breath and hold it as long as is comfortable. As you exhale, your face is relaxing. (Pause.) Your eyes are relaxing. You're breathing slowly … deeply. Your forehead is relaxing. (Pause.) Your jaw is relaxing. (Pause.) Slowly take a deep breath and hold it as long as is comfortable. As you exhale, your chest is relaxing. Your stomach is relaxing. (Pause.) Feel the relaxation going down your back. Your spine is relaxing. You're breathing slowly … deeply. Your arms are relaxing. Your fingers are relaxing. Slowly take a deep breath and hold it as long as is comfortable. As you exhale, feel the relaxation going down your legs. Your feet are relaxing. Feeling very … very peaceful. Breathing slowly … deeply. (Pause for several minutes).

"God is light. God is love. (Pause.) This is your God light protection. (Pause.) Breathing slowly … deeply. Going deeper … and deeper into awareness. Becoming pure mind. (Pause.) Knowing exactly where you are at all times. Knowing exactly what you're doing.

"Slowly take a deep breath and hold it as long as is comfortable. As you exhale, feel yourself relaxing, relaxing, relaxing. Breathe in … two … three … four … five … six … seven … eight. Hold (your breath), two, three, four. Out (exhale), two … three … four … five … six … seven … eight. (Repeat three times.) You're feeling very, very relaxed.

"Concentrate on your mind's eye. Visualize a white light. (Pause.) The light is becoming larger, brighter. Sense the love within the light. (Pause.) Breathing very slowly. Very deeply. Knowing exactly where you are at all times. Knowing exactly what you're doing. *You* are in control. Going deeper ... and deeper ... into a new awareness. Becoming pure mind.

"Concentrate on the mind's eye. Beautiful white images are coming toward you. Listen to their message. (Pause for several minutes or as long as agreed upon.) Mentally bless the images. Thank them for coming. Breathing very slowly ... very deeply. Slowly take a deep breath. You are now coming back. On the count of three, you will open your eyes. One. Your breathing is getting deeper ... stronger. Two. Feeling very, very good. Three. Open your eyes."

*End of meditation.

Group Discussion Checklist

Did the 8-8 Method of Breathing increase your ability to slow your brain waves at will?

Has counting improved your concentration while in meditation?

Has your visualization increased within your mind's eye?

Did the images offer a message?

What, if anything, did you sense or see in your mind's eye?

The following meditation is intentionally very short. It should be memorized until its meaning is fully understood. If you are interrupted unexpectedly, you will be able to return from meditation without startling your physical body. You need only take one long, deep breath and then open your eyes. With practice, it will become a natural response to returning from meditation easily and quickly.

Return from Meditation

"You are now coming back. Take a long, deep breath. Your breathing is getting deeper and stronger. On the count of three, you will open your eyes, feeling very, very good. Breathing in. One. Every day in every way, I'm getting better and better. Your breathing deeper ... stronger. Two. Every day in every way, I'm getting better and better. Three. Open your eyes. Feeling very, very good."

*End of meditation.

Group Discussion Checklist
Have you ever been startled while meditating?
What, if anything, did you do when startled during meditation?
Does taking a deep breath help balance or center your body?

Chapter 4
VISUALIZATION AND PSYCHOMETRY

"Meditation to Increase Visualization" is intended to stimulate the mind's eye. It is intentionally longer, designed to hold one's attention for a longer period of time. The right side of the brain, the intuitive brain, becomes more active. The very act of meditation slows down the brain waves, allowing the right brain to receive information by symbols, images, and emotions.

During meditation, you may or may not see images or symbols on the first try. Some people may need days or months of practice. If an image doesn't spontaneously appear, you will be asked to create images within your mind's eye. This may not seem to be a psychic approach, but it is a necessary step to coax the mind's eye to visualization. Some people are natural clairvoyants. They see images or symbols clearly. Some will not see but will sense an image or object. They are clairsentient. Either way is right if it works for you.

While in meditation, you will be guided to visualize, in the mind's eye, a variety of objects, shapes, colors and to sense the emotion of a scene. This is intended to strengthen the third eye and to read emotions. Movement will be introduced by visualizing different animals moving about a wooded area. By watching the movement, the mind will learn to wait for a scene to unfold until a complete meaning is obtained. The meditation will shift forward and backward in time. This is a preparation for future exercises, such as reviewing childhood memories.

You will be asked to mentally drift up into the clouds. This is intended to encourage the mind to mentally move beyond physical limitations. You will be asked to visualize your own spiritual guidance. You may see a whole or part of an image, a white light, or a glowing illumination or only feel the guide's love and compassion. Don't be discouraged if the images don't spontaneously appear in your mind's eye on the first try. Time and patience will pay off in the end. With practice, you should be able to sense your own spirit guides.

Last but not least, you will be asked to visualize or imagine a person standing at a cottage door. No attempt should be made to create the image of a specific person or loved one. This image should come without any effort. The presence of a specific person or a loved one will be directed by your guides or by a higher spiritual intervention, not by who you want to see or expect that loved one to be. The image may be someone you know, have known in a previous life, or don't know at all. Pay close attention to the message received. It may prove very important in the future. Each section of this meditation is designed to strengthen a different awareness.

Sit up straight with your head upright. Don't cross your arms or legs. Relax your body. Don't make any noise or interrupt the meditation by whispering. Don't leave your seat during a meditation, as this would be disruptive to the other members. Wait until the meditation is over before asking questions. Meditation to Increase Visualization may be prerecorded, or one person may recite the following meditation slowly in a soft, mesmerizing tone of voice.

This meditation can be done by one person alone. He/she will prerecord the meditation and then, with eyes closed, follow the step-by-step meditation.

Meditation to Increase Visualization

"Close your eyes. You're breathing slowly … deeply. Relaxing … relaxing. Mentally ask your guides to stand by for protection, guidance, and direction. (Pause.) Visualize a cloud of white light surrounding your body. God is light. God is love. (Pause.) This is your God light protection. Your forehead is relaxing. Your eyes are relaxing. Slowly, take a deep breath and hold it as long as is comfortable. As you slowly exhale, your neck is relaxing. Feel the relaxation going down your shoulders, down your arms. (Pause.) Your hands are relaxing.

"Slowly take a deep breath and hold it as long as is comfortable. As you slowly exhale, your chest is relaxing. You're breathing slowly ... deeply. Feel the relaxation going down your body. (Pause.) Your body is relaxing ... relaxing. (Pause.) Going deeper ... and deeper in awareness. Becoming pure mind. (Pause.) Knowing exactly where you are at all times. Knowing exactly what you're doing.

"Concentrate on the third eye. In front of you is a red apple. Notice the color. (Pause.) The stem has small leaves. (Pause.) There are dewdrops on the leaves. (Pause.) Next to the apple is a peeled banana. Notice the color ... the texture. (Pause.) You now see a half of a lemon. Notice the bright yellow color. Taste the lemon. (Pause.) Sense the tartness. (Pause.) A butterfly has landed near the lemon. Notice the color of its wings. It walks toward the lemon ... tastes the lemon. Flutters its wings. It didn't like the taste. It's walking away. It stops. Flutters its wings and then flies up toward the clouds.

"You're looking up at the clouds. Feeling lighter and lighter. You are rising up ... up ... up ... toward the clouds. There is an angel to your right. There is an angel to your left. You're rising higher ... and higher. (Pause.) Feel the gentle breeze as it brushes against your face. You're rising higher ... higher. Feeling very relaxed ... very peaceful. Knowing exactly where you are at all times. Knowing exactly what you're doing. (Pause.) You are in control.

"Below you see treetops. You're drifting down ... down ... into a beautiful wooded area. The autumn leaves have turned gold and orange. Listen to the leaves rustle in the wind. (Pause.)

"Ahead of you is a path. There is an angel to your right. An angel to your left. You're walking down the path. Smell the humid earth beneath you. Listen to the leaves as they crunch beneath your feet. The sunlight peeks between the leaves. You step into the sunlight. Feel the warmth of the sun. (Pause.)

"Ahead of you is a squirrel. It bristles its tail and then scampers across the path. It stops. Looks at you. Notice the wisdom in its eyes. It bristles its tail and scampers into the woods.

"Two deer are standing on the path. You drift closer. They look at you. Notice the gentleness in their eyes. They twitch their ears, listening. You move closer. See the softness of their fur. The beauty of their bodies. The large deer turns, looks at you, and then nudges the doe. They turn and slowly walk away. Notice the white tip of their tails as they walk down the path. They move slowly between the trees until they are gone.

"You are drifting down the path. Your angels are beside you. Ahead of you is a robin perched in a tree. You move closer. The robin flutters its wings … nods its head as a welcome. (Pause.) Notice the soft feathers. The bright orange of its breast. (Pause.) It hops up a branch. You see a nest of baby robins. Watch. Enjoy. (Pause.) Mentally bless them. Thank them for coming.

"You're following the angels down the path. Ahead of you is a small, wooden bridge. You're moving closer … and closer. You are walking across the wood slats of the bridge. You stop … look over the railing. Below sparkling water flows over large rocks. (Pause.) Watch the ripple of the water as it flows under the bridge. Listen to the sound as the water splashes against the rocks. Feel the cool droplets of water splashing against your face. Slowly take a deep breath. Breathing in the fresh air. (Pause.) Feeling very, very peaceful … very content.

"You're moving across the bridge toward a small cottage. There's a person standing in the doorway. You move closer. The person beckons you to come closer. You move closer. The person welcomes you with an embrace. (Pause.) Listen to the words of wisdom. (Pause for several minutes or as long as agreed upon.) You embrace the person. Say good-bye and then return slowly toward the small bridge.

"You're moving over the bridge. You step off the bridge, climb down to the water's edge, and sit on a large rock. Listen to the sound of water splashing against the rocks. (Pause.) Feel the cool water as it splashes against your face. (Pause.) You are returning to the path. At the edge of the wooded area you see brilliant sunlight. The angels drift ahead of you. They open their arms and a brilliant burst of light illuminates the path. Their arms glisten like shimmering wings. You step into the sunlight. Feel the warmth of the sun. Breathing in the energy of the sunlight. (Pause.) Mentally, thank your angels for guiding you in meditation. (Pause.) See them nod. Feel the love they send. Listen to their words of wisdom. (Pause for several minutes or as long as agreed upon.)

"Breathing deeply … slowly. On the count of three, you will open your eyes feeling very, very good. Coming back. Your breathing is getting deeper … stronger. Coming back. One. Every day in every way, I'm getting better and better. (Pause.) Breathing deeper … stronger.

Two. Every day in every way, I'm getting better and better. (Pause.) Three. Your eyes are open. Feeling very, very good."
*End of meditation.

Repeat this meditation often until you have accomplished visualizing objects and movement and sensing emotions. With repetition, you may expect images of your angels or guides to become more distinct. As your enlightenment expands, your higher self—your super-subconscious mind—may present messages or guidance relevant to your soul's spiritual development. This will occur as a thought in your head or an idea of proper judgment. Give great consideration to the message and its meaning. Don't be disappointed if communication with your guides doesn't take place immediately. It takes time and practice to awaken the senses and understand the spiritual messages.

After each meditation, the group is encouraged to discuss their visual experiences. Often strange, unusual symbols appear in the mind's eye. You may hesitate to mention your own symbols, because they seem comical, weird, or unusually strange. Don't hesitate. The universe is full of unusual energies. Offer your experiences. Discussion is an important part of each lesson. It will lead to a broader understanding of your symbols and will help others understand their own symbols.

Group Discussion Checklist
Has your ability to visualize within the mind's eye increased?
Did you see colors and movement? If so, what colors appeared most prominent?
Did your mouth salivate when you tasted the lemon?
Did you mentally communicate with an animal?
How did you feel when your thoughts drifted up into the clouds?
Did you see or sense your guardian angels or guides?
What, if any, strange symbols or images did you see?
Did you receive a personal message?
Have you recorded your personal message for future use?
Discuss your message if it's not too personal.

The following combined meditation is intentionally longer. The counting of numbers will help one's concentration. The extended time in meditation will allow the brain waves to reach a deeper level of awareness. This will increase one's ability to visualize images, colors, and movement.

Meditation 8-8 Method of Breathing and Meditation to Increase Visualization

"Close your eyes. Mentally visualize a cloud of light surrounding your body. God is light. God is love. (Pause.) This is your God light protection. Slowly ... take a deep breath and hold it as long as is comfortable. As you exhale, release all your cares ... all your problems. Feel the relaxation going down your body. (Pause.) Breathing very deeply ... very slowly. Going deeper ... and deeper ... into awareness. Slowly take a deep breath and hold it as long as is comfortable. As you exhale, you are relaxing ... relaxing ... relaxing. Breathe in ... two ... three ... four ... five ... six ... seven ... eight. Hold (your breath), two ... three ... four. Out (exhale), two ... three ... four ... five ... six ... seven ... eight. (Repeat at least three times or more if necessary.)

"You're feeling very, very relaxed. Concentrate on your mind's eye. Visualize a white light. (Pause.) The light is becoming larger ... brighter. Sense the love within the light. (Pause.) Breathing very slowly. Very deeply. Going deeper ... and deeper ... into awareness. Knowing exactly where you are at all times. Knowing exactly what you're doing. (Pause.) You are in control. Going deeper ... and deeper into a new awareness. Becoming pure mind. Mentally ask your guides to stand by for protection, guidance, and direction. (Pause.)

"Your forehead is relaxing. Your eyes are relaxing. Slowly take a deep breath and hold it as long as is comfortable. As you exhale, your neck is relaxing. Feel the relaxation going down your shoulders, down your arms. Slowly take a deep breath and hold it as long as is comfortable. As you exhale, your body is relaxing ... relaxing ... relaxing. (Pause.) Going deeper ... and deeper ... in awareness. Becoming pure mind. (Pause.) Knowing exactly where you are at all times. Knowing exactly what you're doing.

"Concentrate on the third eye. In front of you is a red apple. Notice the color. (Pause.) See the stem with small leaves. (Pause.) Notice the dewdrops on the leaves. Next to the apple is a peeled banana. Notice the color ... the texture. (Pause.) You now see a half of a lemon. Notice the bright yellow color. Taste the lemon. (Pause.) Sense the tartness. (Pause.) A butterfly has landed near the lemon. Notice the color of its wings. It walks toward the lemon … tastes the lemon. Flutters its wings. It didn't like the taste. It slowly walks away. It stops. Flutters its wings and then flies up toward the clouds.

"You're looking up at the clouds. You're feeling lighter … and lighter. You are rising up … up … up … toward the clouds. There is an angel to your right. An angel to your left. You're rising higher and higher. Feel the gentle breeze as it brushes against your face. You're feeling very relaxed, very peaceful. Knowing exactly where you are at all times. Knowing exactly what you're doing. (Pause.) You are in control.

"Below you see treetops. You're drifting down … down … into a beautiful wooded area. (Pause.) Notice the autumn leaves. The sunlit gold and orange leaves rustle in the wind. (Pause.)

"Ahead of you is a path. There is an angel to your right. An angel to your left. You are walking down the path. Smell the humid earth beneath you. Listen to the leaves as they crunch beneath your feet. The sunlight peeks between the leaves. You step into the sunlight. Feel the warmth of the sun. (Pause.)

"Ahead of you is a squirrel. It bristles its tail and then scampers across the path. It stops. Looks at you. Notice the wisdom in its eyes. It bristles its tail and scampers into the woods.

"Two deer are standing on the path. You drift closer. They look at you. Notice the gentleness in their eyes. They twitch their ears, listening. You move closer. See the softness of their fur. The beauty of their bodies. The large deer turns … looks at you and then nudges the doe. They turn and slowly walk away. Notice the white tip of their tails as they walk down the path. They move slowly between the trees until they are gone.

"You're drifting down the path. Your angels are beside you. Ahead of you is a robin perched in a tree. You move closer. The robin flutters its wings … nods its head as a welcome. Notice the soft feathers. The bright orange of its breast. (Pause.) It hops up a branch. You see a nest of baby robins. Watch. Enjoy. (Pause for one minute or as decided.) Mentally bless them.

"You are following the angels down the path. Ahead of you is a small, wooden bridge. You're moving closer … closer. You are walking across the wood slats of the bridge. You stop … look over the railing.

Below sparkling water flows over large rocks. (Pause.) Watch the ripple of the water as it flows under the bridge. Listen to the sound as the water splashing against the rocks. Feel the cool droplets of water splashing against your face. You're breathing slowly … deeply. Breathing in the fresh air. (Pause.) You feel very peaceful, very content.

"You're returning across the bridge. You step off the bridge and climb down to the water's edge and sit on a large rock. Listen to the sound of water splashing against the rocks. (Pause.) Feel the cool water splashing against your face. (Pause.) You are returning to the path. At the edge of the wooded area, you see brilliant sunlight. The angels drift ahead of you. They open their arms, and a burst of brilliant light illuminates the path. The glowing vibrations from their arms glisten like shimmering wings. You step into the sunlight. Feel the warmth of the sun. Breathing in the energy of the sunlight. Mentally thank your angels for guiding you in meditation. See them nod. Feel the love they send. (Pause for several minutes.)

"Breathing deeply … slowly. On the count of three, you will open your eyes. Your breathing is getting deeper … stronger. Coming back. One. Every day in every way, I'm getting better and better. (Pause.) Breathing deeper, stronger. Two. Every day in every way, I'm getting better and better. (Pause.) Three. Your eyes are open. Feeling very, very good."

*End of meditation.

Group Discussion Checklist

Did combining the meditations improve your ability to meditate?

Did counting down help your concentration?

Is your breathing more controlled when counting down?

Do you find yourself breathing more deeply and calmly?

Each time you have meditated, have you noticed an improvement in seeing within the mind's eye?

Did you feel or sense your angels or guides?

Which meditation gave the best results?

Psychometry

Psychometry is performed by concentrating on the forehead—the third eye—to read, see, or sense vibrations surrounding an object. The reading may be done with eyes open or closed. Each reading may require a different method, because each object or client is different.

Psychometry is the ability to read particles of energy surrounding an object, such as jewelry, clothing, pictures, etc., by touch. The object may be as small as a ring or as large as the wall of a building. The reader will hold the object and feel the vibrations within the object. All objects are imprinted with vibrations that hold memories of the owner's daily experiences or past events. Those vibrations can be seen or sensed within the mind's eye as images or symbols that illustrate a meaning.

When holding an object, you may see or sense a clear or blurred image; a part of the body, such as an arm or a leg; or complex images. Sometimes the image moves about to dramatize a situation. Or you may see part of a scene, such as a tree or fence, or sense a particular season. Seasons often refer to the time in which an incident had or will occur. Those images, when correctly analyzed, depict a situation in which the owner of the object took part.

Group Discussion Checklist

Do you sense or see images within the mind's eye?

Can you create an image in the mind's eye?

What images, if any, have you already seen? Discuss their potential meaning.

When your eyes are closed, are you able to concentrate more easily?

Protection

Each psychometry reading should begin with a prayer or request for protection. You may mentally or verbally recite a prayer, imagine the God light or white light, or mentally call upon your guardian angels or guides for protection, guidance, and directions. Using spiritual protection brings a sense of confidence, relaxes your body, and makes the process of psychometry easier. Protection may be sensed or seen in the mind's eye as God light, white light, angels, guides, circles of light, sparkles, colors, or just a positive feeling. Even if you don't see or sense your guides, be assured they are present, especially if you have a sincere desire to use the art of psychometry for good. Any prayer may be used, but the best prayer comes from the heart.

A Suggested Prayer
"I ask my guides to stand by for protection, guidance, and the very highest spiritual assistance I am capable of using."

Notice the prayer asks for "the very highest spiritual assistance I am capable of using." If you had asked only for the "very highest," would you be capable of using what you do not yet understand? The spiritual realm has many dimensions that we, as humans, will not understand until we have passed over into the spirit world. Be sure to ask only for that which you are capable of using or understanding. Be aware of how you pray and for what purpose.

Group Discussion Checklist
Do you see or sense the white light when requesting spiritual protection?
Do you see or sense a guide or angel when asking for protection?
Share with the class your own specific prayer for protection.

Reading an Object
Before reading an object, you may intuitively rub your hands together to create a static. This will make your hands more sensitive, thus easier to connect with the object's vibrations. Select an object, such as a ring, jewelry, eyeglasses, or an article of clothing. An object worn daily by one person will hold more energy vibrations than an object seldom used. It's best to begin with a metal object. Metal tends to hold a stronger vibration; therefore, it is easier to read. Beginners should use an object that has had only one owner and has been worn by only one owner. Those vibrations will be clear because they are not intermingled with the previous owner's energy.

Antiques are more complex. A novice should not begin by reading an antique piece of jewelry. An antique that has been handed down from generation to generation will have generations of memories imprinted in its vibrations. An heirloom ring that once belonged to Grandma will carry Grandma's vibrations or Great-Grandma's vibrations as well as the present owner's. The reader will get a mixed reading because the vibrations surrounding the heirloom will display symbols belonging to the grandma, great-grandma, and current owner. Grandma's past tragedy might be incorrectly read as the current owner's tragedy and could impose needless worry and stress. The reader is responsible if he/she creates needless stress or worry upon another. Through my forty years of communication with the spirit world, I now believe when we cross over into the next dimension, we will face and/or relive all that we have caused to others. If this is true, then that alone is a good reason to give an accurate, honest reading.

Keys should not be read, as they have far too many vibrations to be read accurately. Keys carried together will have mingled vibrations of home, office, car, or other family members who have used those keys. It's difficult to target a specific key's vibrations without it being affected by the other keys' vibrations.

Photographs, letters, and greeting cards, especially with signatures, carry strong vibrations. The reader should hold the paper face down so the signature or face is not visible. Seeing the person's face or signature could influence the reading. Psychometry is done by reading vibrations and should not be influenced by personal knowledge.

Group Discussion Checklist

What metal jewelry or holiday objects would be easy to read? Why?

Name several objects that are good candidates for psychometry.

What kind of greeting cards can be used? Why?

Suggest where to find signatures to be read.

Bring several family photographs to the next class for a psychometry reading.

Left Hand

Start by holding the object to be read in the left hand. The nervous system crosses from the left hand to the right brain. The right side of the brain—the intuitive brain—can sense a situation, use intuition, see spatial concepts, and visualize images. Therefore, when the left hand connects with an object, the right brain is triggered into action, and the vibrations can be read more easily. Practice with either or both hands until you find which works best for you. However, there may come a time when you sense a need to switch hands in the middle of a reading. Remember, there are no set rules.

Switching hands may occur because:

- The owner of the object has or once had an injured hand.
- The need to switch hands may indicate a concern for the injured hand.
- The message refers to a specific hand for its reading, identifying the object's owner.
- The reader senses a need to switch hands while the reading for unknown reasons.
- The reader may feel a need to use both hands while reading the object.

Symbols

The reader may see or sense many different symbols within the mind's eye. Each symbol is a vibratory imprint, a way of identifying a person, place, or circumstance surrounding the object being read. Symbols are not universally the same. People apply different connotations on a symbol due to personal circumstances, past experiences, religious beliefs, or ethnic or cultural customs. While holding an object to be read, expect unusual or strange symbols to appear. The meaning of symbols will change as the group discusses the checklist to identify how another person might read the same symbols.

Some people read symbols as a clairvoyant; they see images within the mind's eye. Some read as a clairaudient; they hear or know the message as a thought within the head. Some read by sensing the vibrations of the object. They are clairsentient. With practice, you can learn to use all three senses with equal proficiency.

Group Discussion Checklist

What unusual symbols have you seen in your mind's eye? What do you think they mean?

What symbols might have a different ethnic or cultural meaning?

Do you see or sense symbols? Or do you know the answer but don't know why?

What Improves Psychometry

Through years of experience, I have found the sincere desire to help another person often triggers a mechanism in the brain that makes psychometry easier. Honesty seems to create a positive energy and appears to enhance the brain's ability to be more keenly aware.

What Obstructs Psychometry

If the reader becomes negative or doubts his or her own ability, the flow of positive energy is interrupted. Any form of negativity, whether it is self-doubt or tension, can prevent the reader from tuning into the object's vibrations. Negative thoughts coming from either the reader or the client can stop the flow of information. Avoid thinking or saying, "I can't do it." Repeat to yourself, "I will see." Or, "I can see." Positive affirmation relaxes the physical body, making the reading of an object easier.

Group Discussion Checklist

Discuss how doubts can stop the flow of energy during a reading.
Do you relax when you know you are right?
Do you feel tense when things are not going smoothly?
Do you feel uneasy when another person lies?
How does tension affect your physical health and body?
How can another person's lies weigh heavily on your mind?
What other things can obstruct a reading? Give examples.

What Blocks a Reading

The client may unknowingly block a reading by merely folding his or her hands across the chest. The act of protecting in a defiant manner sets up a dense energy field around a client's body. The reader will find it difficult to penetrate the client's aura when access is denied. Enlightened psychics who are spiritually aware may not want to penetrate a negative force field. It would be of no value if the client isn't ready to accept or believe the information given. If the reader either lies or falsifies a story to impress the client, the reader's body will react to his or her own deception. Any intentional falsification creates a dense barrier, blocking and/or confusing the interpretation of the message.

Group Discussion Checklist

Have you ever witnessed a stubborn person fold his or her hands across the chest in defiance? Did you intuitively feel a barrier?

Have you ever felt a negative person's energy? Explain.

Have you ever felt a very spiritual person's energy? Explain.

Truth and Responsibility

Psychometry is not to be taken lightly. There should be no ego. Don't dim your aura light by intentionally giving inaccurate information just to boost your ego. When giving a reading, consider the proverb, "What so ever you sow, so shall you reap." Honesty is very important, because when you and I pass over into the next dimension, we enter the dimension corresponding to the radiance of our auras. Our spiritual essence is our validation.

Feeling Vibrations

Sometimes a cold chill can be felt on or near the hands when doing psychometry. The chill may be a vibrational change in the atmosphere, the energy of a memory, or the presence of a spirit. A spirit's presence may be felt as a slightly cool breeze or as cold as if you stuck your hand into a freezer.

While performing psychometry, a clairsentient might sense an injury the owner of that object had or is currently experiencing. The client's injury is usually sensed but not felt physically. However, there may come a time when the reader actually feels a portion of the client's pain. When this happens, the reader has empathized with the client. This discomfort usually leaves as soon as the reading ends. If, after the reading has ended, the discomfort remains, those vibrations should be released.

The reader may release the discomfort by:

- visualizing the discomfort rising up off the body.
- visualizing the God light lifting any remaining vibrations.
- raising his or her hands up as if pulling off a sweater to release the vibrations.
- allowing the body to respond with a slight shiver or shudder as the vibrations are released.

- mentally suggesting, "I release *these* memory vibrations. I am releasing. I am releasing."
- breathing in the God light to cleanse the body.
- using any method intuitively received to release vibrations.

Group Discussion Checklist

Have you felt the presence of a spirit as a chill or wisp of cool air?

Have you felt a spirit touch or actually pick up your hair?

Have you felt the hair on your arms or the back of your neck rise in the presence of a spirit?

Have you experienced the presence of a spirit?

Have you empathized with another person's pain?

Do you feel despondent when a negative person stays in your presence for a long time?

What method do you use to release empathy?

Do you breathe in the God light to replenish your body with positive energy?

Rise above Emotions

When reading an object, there may come time when the reader observes a tragic scene as seen through the eyes of the object's owner. If the event is violent or frightening, the reader may find it difficult to separate his or her own emotions from the scene. When this happens, the reader should remove him or herself from the scene. Imagine hovering over the scene. Observe rather than interact with it. It's very important to learn all aspects of psychometry and how to separate from any emotional experience. If the reader becomes emotionally involved, he/she should mentally recite the following: "I am rising above. I am lifting up out of the scene. I feel no emotion. I am *only observing*. I am *only observing* . I am leaving this scene. I release *this* to the God light. I am leaving this scene."

Group Discussion Checklist

Are you empathetic toward another person's pain?

Do you sense or actually feel another person's pain?

How do you release another person's pain from your energy field?

Can you now release yourself from the emotion of a tragic situation?

Sources of Information

Information may come from many different sources, depending upon the reader's psychic ability and spiritual awareness.

The conscious mind usually receives information directly from the vibrations surrounding the object being read. The quality of the reading will depend upon the reader's intent to reach the highest spiritual guidance he/she is capable of using. If the reader is spiritually inclined, the reading may be done with both the conscious mind and spiritual assistance at the same time.

Thought vibrations and the object's vibrations may appear in the mind's eye as symbols and/or images. There may come a time that a client's thoughts, desires, or fears are so concentrated that they override the object's vibrations. The reader may think he/she is reading the object when, in fact, the reader is tuning into the client's present thoughts or desires. The reader is responsible to sense if he/she is reading the client's thoughts or the object's vibration.

For example, the reader may tune into a young girl's bracelet and images of a bride appear. The reader may alert the girl a marriage is in her future. But did the reader tune into the bracelet's vibrations? Not necessarily. The reader may have tuned into the young girl's desire for marriage, misinterpreting her thoughts as if they were certainties about to occur. It will take practice before one can intuitively sense which vibrations are the client's thoughts and which are attached to the object being read.

Personal guides often assist in psychometry. The more spiritually motivated the reader is, the easier it will be to attain spiritual knowledge. The reader may call upon his or her own personal guides or the client's personal guides to receive information. Often, the reader's guides will confer with the client's guides. This information will be conveyed to the reader in a mental message or a visual image within the mind's eye. When spiritual intervention is involved, the reader will sense a peaceful feeling or will simply know the information is accurate. By practicing psychometry often, the reader will become familiar with the spirit guides.

Through years of contact with the spirit world, it is my belief that angels don't usually give messages during a psychometry reading. Angels and guides have been allocated different agendas for servicing humankind. Angels protect, guide, and/or create synchronization and coincidence to safeguard a human body and to ensure spiritual progress. Angels are so powerful they can physically intervene in an accident to protect a person from harm. Angels may give personal messages (not necessarily through a psychometry reading) by projecting a thought in the person's head. An idea may suddenly seem to come from out of the blue. It is the angel's way of alerting a person to a specific situation.

While reading psychometry, there may come a time when the reader suddenly spouts words of wisdom he or she did not know or had intended to say. It may be the angel's way to help either the reader or the client to gain spiritual enlightenment. Therefore, it is rare but not impossible that information can come directly from an angel while performing psychometry.

Group Discussion Checklist

Have you ever received a warning by your guides or an angel? What did you do?

Have you sensed a need to do something but didn't know where the idea came from?

Share any stories of a person receiving help from an angel.

Spirits

Most ghosts or wandering spirits are souls who have not yet crossed over into the God light. They usually are not dangerous or evil. They are just unaware of the God consciousness. Some spirits, good or bad, may see the glow of the reader's aura and be drawn in by the psychic energy the reader is giving off. However, if the reader is egotistical or not honest, his or her aura would not be clear and bright. A dull aura can attract troublesome spirits. Like draws like. Thus, a troubled reader might draw a troubled spirit while in the process of psychometry.

Some spirits and ghosts hang around just to be meddlesome. They enjoy sending frightening messages. With practice, the reader should be able to sense a negative spirit by the irritating or dull energy it gives off. When reader recognizes the spirits' or ghosts' intentions, he or she should ask them to leave. Or the reader may mentally set a spirit aside with love and white light. Remember, spirits and ghosts are just people existing in a different dimension. Treat them with respect but be firm that they leave. It's the reader's responsibility to know if the message has come from the object's vibrations or a nosy spirit.

Spirits and ghosts move about on thought patterns. Therefore, they move as fast as they think. They are where the think they are. They go where they want to be. The reader may mentally bless them and then mentally project the thought, "You will see your guardian angels. They will direct you to the God light. Go to the God light." Most of the time but not always, the spirit will move on that thought.

If a mischievous spirit or ghost does not leave immediately, the reader should mentally project a firm, authoritative thought, "*Step back! Go to the God light.*" Since the spirit moves on thought patterns, it will or may be subject to the reader's thoughts.

When the reader senses a mischievous spirit or ghost, he/she should:

- mentally request the spirit or ghost to go to the God light.
- not send out any fear of the spirit.
- visualize a blanket of light covering the spirit or ghost and then direct it to rise into the light.
- mentally converse with the spirit or ghost and explain it is dead and should go to the God light.
- use any message you intuitively receive to help the spirit or ghost to the light.

Group Discussion Checklist

Have you ever sensed a spirit or a ghost?

Have you received a message from a mischievous spirit?

Can you sense a meddling spirit?

Have you ever felt a spirit's or ghost's presence near a particular object?

Do you now treat a spirit with respect? Are you willing to help guide them to the light?

Knowing that most spirits are not evil, how has your attitude toward spirits changed?

Discuss the meaning of "like draws like."

Contact a Deceased Loved One

Psychometry can be used to contact a deceased person by holding an object that once belonged to the deceased. The images or symbols seen in the mind's eye may be vibratory memories of the deceased or the actual presence of the spirit. A spirit may hover close to communicate an important message or merely to comfort the living. Just because a spirit is communicating doesn't mean that message is accurate. The information may be interesting or partly true but not necessarily accurate. It is only that spirit's interpretation of what had occurred when it owned the object. The spirit may be relaying information based on its own previous life. It may have passed over recently and have not yet learned the true meaning of its existence. Only messages from guides, highly evolved spirits, or spiritual masters should be relied upon as accurate.

When the reader contacts a deceased person, he or she should present the information with calmness and purpose. Be sure the client doesn't fear the spirit. The very act of fear sets off a negative vibration and can block communication with a loved one. It's the reader's responsibility to inform the client that spirits are just people existing in another dimension.

Group Discussion Checklist

Have you ever sensed a deceased loved one in the room with you?

How do you recognize the presence of a spirit?

Did you mentally or verbally acknowledge the loved one's presence?

Smell

While performing psychometry, unusual odors or fragrances may manifest on or near the object being read. A fragrance that once belonged to a deceased father may appear, emitting his favorite scent (i.e., a pipe or cigarette). A female spirit may emit a scent of perfume or a favorite food she once cooked. The spirit may discharge a personal scent as proof of its presence. When the scent is recognized, the reader should mentally or verbally acknowledge that spirit's presence. Bless the spirit. Thank it for coming.

In psychometry, it's possible but rare that obnoxious odors are smelled. This may happen if the reader is helping the police to find a missing person. Sometimes the scent of a dead body or toxic fumes may emanate from the object being read. Odors usually emphasize or clarify what had once occurred on or near the object being read.

Group Discussion Checklist

Have you smelled perfume or cigarette smoke reminiscent of a friend or family member?

Did you mentally or verbally acknowledge the spirit's presence?

What, if any, paranormal scent have you smelled that did not have a physical cause?

Was the scent isolated in only one area or near only one person?

Antiques

Some antiques may be impressed with strong vibrations that cause the antique to appear haunted. The reader may see in his or her mind's eye a scene in which the object was once involved. The reader may see moving images or an event in progress. If the scene is tragic, the reader may feel or sense the emotions or fear of the scene. However, in some cases, it's not the spirit who is haunting the object. It is merely energy emanating from the object, depicting a rerun of an event.

Some spirits enter the light and then return to visit a family member or check on their possessions. The reader might encounter such a spirit when performing psychometry on antique furniture, photographs, or antiquated objects. The current owner of the object may believe the antique is haunted, but in truth, the spirit may only be visiting or may want to convey a message. Most spirits don't come with evil intentions. They don't intend to frighten the owner of the object. They are just a person existing in a different dimension.

Spirits sometimes hang around something familiar. In its inability to clear its thoughts, it may think it still owns the antique, so it remains earthbound, determined to watch over its prized possession. Such spirits might become attached to an object or antique or even roam within a house. The client may think the spirit is haunting the antique or the house when, in fact, it is the spirit who is haunted by its own inability to cross over into the God light.

Spirits have been known to frighten the living. Often it's their way to attract attention, to call for help. The reader should mentally communicate with it, bless it, and offer guidance by imagining the God light as a way to cross over into the next dimension. Before purchasing an antique, handle it and feel it. Be sure it doesn't come with spirits or negative memory vibrations.

Group Discussion Checklist

Have you sensed a spirit near an antique?

Do you have an object or antique you think is haunted?

Has a friend told you of a haunted antique?

Have you encountered a spirit attached to an antique? How did you recognize it?

Clear Vibrations

After performing psychometry, the reader may wish to clear his or her aura of any remaining vibrations. This can be done in many different ways:

- Visualize any vibrations being lifted off the body.
- Recite a prayer, asking God to lift the vibrations.
- Mentally cover the body in God light to clear vibrations.
- Apply short, hand movements across the chest and shoulders to brush away particles of energy left on your aura.
- Move the hands in an upward motion to release vibrations. When moving the hands up over the head, as if taking off a sweater, a slight shudder or natural quiver of the body often accompanies the cleansing. When the hands are raised above the head, the vibrations are released more easily into the atmosphere.
- Request the vibrations be absorbed by the God light.

Chakras

The human body has seven major nerve centers called chakras. They are psychic doors that open to spiritual awareness. Chakras naturally open during a psychic reading. The reader may choose to close the chakras after the reading has ended.

- A chakra will close when the reader mentally suggests, "My chakras are now closed."
- The reader may move his or her hands downward from head to chest to close the chakras.
- The mere fact of knowing the chakras are closed will close the chakras.
- Each person will find his or her own way to clear vibrations, whether it is a simple prayer or a message intuitively received.
- It isn't necessary to close the chakras after an average reading.

Exercise 1. Psychometry

Each member should bring several objects to class for a psychometry reading. The object may be one they own or that of a family member or a friend. The object may be a piece of jewelry, article of clothing, or any object. For best results, the object should belong to only one owner and worn by only that owner. The owner of the object (the client) need not be present during the reading. The group will pair up in partners. It's best to select a partner with whom you have little or no knowledge. Each person will take a turn at reading the other person's object.

The reader may do any or all of the following:

- Sit in a comfortable chair. Spine should be straight. Eyes may be open or closed.
- Recite a prayer (mentally or aloud) for protection or call upon God, white light, angels, or guides for assistance and protection.
- Rub the hands together to create a static energy to kick-start a connection with the object's energy.
- Hold the object in the left hand. Feel it. Move it within the finger. Try the other hand.
- Tune into the object until the vibrations have formed images or symbols in the mind's eye.
- Start by voicing an impression of what you are receiving.
- Don't use logic.
- Expect images or symbols to appear in the mind's eye.
- Report each symbol even if it seems silly or absurd. That symbol may have a meaning to the client.
- Ask the client what a specific symbol means to him or her.
- Combine the images and symbols as they relate to the scene.
- Mentally ask your guides to show an answer to a specific question.
- Don't tell yourself, "I can't do this." Negative thoughts close down the psychic communication.
- **Never *predict a death*.** Some symbols could be misread and misinterpret a future death. This would cause needless worry and heartache. Psychometry should not be taken lightly.

The client may do any of the following:

- Do not interrupt the reader as this will stop or interfere with the flow of communication.
- Acknowledge a direct hit specific only to the client or the object.

Choose a partner. Begin psychometry reading.

Group Discussion Checklist
Did you see or sense images, symbols, or movement?
Did your partner help by confirming each direct hit?
How many direct hits did you have?
What did you consider a direct hit?
How did you analyze a symbol?
Which symbol or image did you find most interesting?
Discuss unusual symbols.
Prepare for the next class by bringing signed greeting cards or letters.

Exercise 2. Read Signature Vibrations

Reading signature vibrations can be done before class begins or as a group project. Each person will bring several signed greeting cards to class. It's best if the signature is signed in cursive rather than print. The flow of curved letters is more revealing and holds more vibrations than stiff, printed letters. The group will divide up into partners, a reader and a client. Select a partner who has little knowledge of you, your family, or friends. The less you know about a person, the less chance of using logic in your reading. A reading should be intuitive, not based on logic.

The reader will hold the signed card with one or both hands. The eyes may be open or closed. Finger the card. Study the signature to get a feel of the writing. Tune into the emotions of the signature. The reader should tell the client what images or symbols are appearing in the mind's eye.

Another option is to read the card only through the senses. In this case, the reader must not look at the signature. He or she should not know if the signature belongs to a man or a woman. The card is placed face down. The reader will move his or her hand slowly over the card or touch the signature while tuning into the card's vibrations. The reader may sense or see, in the mind's eye, a person or an emotion that occurred at the time the writer signed the card.

If the partner has no greeting cards, he or she may write a famous or well-known person's name on a sheet of paper. The paper is placed face down in the same manner as a greeting card.

To test your skills at home, select several greeting cards that family or friends have signed. You have seen their signatures many times but have not read the true emotion of that signature. Your normal eyes did not see what your third eye can see. Turn all the cards face down. Read only one card at a time. Slide your fingers under one card. Feel the signature. Symbols, images, or a scene may appear in the mind's eye. The signature may emit a series of symbols or emotions that occurred at the time the card was signed. After you have analyzed the meaning, check the name to verify if you have correctly identified the signer. This exercise will strengthen your psychic ability and will be helpful in learning more about your own symbols and images.

Symbols

When performing psychometry, symbols may appear in the mind's eye. Symbols are not universally the same. Personal experience often color the way a symbol is interpreted. In time, each person will incorporate his or her own symbols while doing psychometry. The group does not need to review each and every symbol; however, since the subconscious mind remembers what it hears, it would be wise to review some symbols. It's similar to learning to spell a word. Once it is heard, spelled, and learned, the mind can recall it more easily. A discussion of some of the symbols is advised.

The most commonly used symbols are listed below:

Clock
A clock may appear in the mind's eye to determine when an event has, or will, occur. Use the hands on a clock as a guide.

12:00 pm (noon) refers to the present time. Therefore, 12:00 pm means an event is now occurring.

9:00 am occurs before noon. Therefore, 9:00 am means a future event will be coming.

11:00 am is nearer to 12:00 noon. Therefore, 11:00 am means a future event will occur soon.

1:00 pm is past noon. 1:00 pm refers to a recently passed event.

3.00 pm is farther away from noon. Therefore, 3:00 pm indicates a past events, but further in the past.

Calendar

A calendar may depict the month or year an event has or will occur. In the mind's eye, allow the pages of the calendar to flip forward for future time, or backward for a past event. Wait until the pages stop or a glow highlights a specific month and/or year.

Location

A glow may appear on a specific place on the map. This will indicate the location that an event has or will occur.

Season

The image of a season such as, winter, summer, spring, or fall, may appear in the mind's eye. This will indicate the time period when an occurrence has or will take place.

Holiday

A specific holiday may appear in the mind's eye. This will indicate the holiday in which an event has or will occur. Combine all symbols to determine the location and time of an event,.

Person

The reader may see or sense a person in the mind's eye. The distance that the person appears determines the length of time the contact has or will be made. Use the clock as a guide to measure before or after an event.

A person standing on the left side (such as before noon as shown on a clock) indicates before the incident will occur. Left side is a future meeting.

A person standing on the right (after noon) indicates the incident has already occurred.

A person appears very close and to the left indicates the person will meet soon.

A person appears very close and to right (after noon). This indicates a meeting will take place soon.

Person appears very close and in the center. This meeting or person exists in present time.

Person appears far away. The further the distance, the more time will elapse before the meeting will take place.

Small person. The size of a person signifies the importance. The smaller the size, the least insignificant..

Person turning his or her back to the reader. This person doesn't want to reveal his or her self. The person refuses to face a situation.

Pioneer. A person who may or had started business. Such as pioneered a business.

Person pushed in a wheelchair. A person being pushed because of his or her own weakness. A person who is unable to stand up to a situation. Or, it can mean a physical invalid.

Face

The face may show specific or prominent features that identify the person.

A whole face that is very close symbolizes an immediate meeting.

A face that is farther away. This person will be met sometime the future. Or, this person was seen a long time ago.

Angry face indicate an angry person. A forewarning to prevent a difficult meeting or circumstance.

Face crying. Sadness. Combine symbols to determine a reason for the sorrow.

Face laughing. Happiness.

Face peeking. Curiosity. Shyness. Afraid to come forward.

Hands holding a head. Worry. Concern.

Covering a face. A person who is shamed, afraid to face a situation, or does not want to be read.

Hands holding back of a neck. Someone is a pain in the neck.

Head appears dizzy. Person is confused.

Nose

A nose. Someone is sticking his or her nose into another person's affairs.

An injured nose. Beware of health or facial injury. Or, will be hurt by interfering in another person's affairs. A warning not to stick your nose in another person's business.

Ears

Ears. Someone is listening.

Hand extended behind the ear. Listen more closely.

Hand covering ear. A person who is refusing to listen, or does not want to hear.

Eyes

Within the eyes can be seen the soul of the person.

Familiar eyes. Identify the person by the eyes. Could be a present or past life person.

Crying tears. Sadness.

Eyes that are straining to see. A need to look more closely at a situation.

An injured eye. A warning to protect one's self from injury.

Eyeglasses

Eyeglasses indicate a need to see more clearly. May need glasses.

Wearing eyeglasses. A need to change eyeglasses. Or, a person who is currently wearing glasses.

Dirty eyeglasses. A person does not see a situation clearly.

Wiping eyeglasses clean. A need to look more clearly at a situation.

Binoculars. A need to focus on a situation. Look in depth. Someone is watching from a distance.

Hand

A hand reaching toward you. You may receive a helping hand.

Hand showing palmistry lines. Read the lines as a palmist.

A hand giving money. May receive a gift of money. A situation regarding money may be presented.

Aura Colors surrounding a head or body

Clear, bright, clean colors indicate a positive color.

Blurry, dismal, or dirty colors indicate a negative color.

Yellow, clear and bright, indicates wisdom and thinking.

Green indicates a peaceful person or a healer.

Blue is a spiritual color.

Purple indicates a spiritual power.

Purple, dark and muddy, indicates an unprincipled power.

Black or gray indicates a dismal attitude or negative thoughts.

Baby

Holding a baby. Someone has a baby or an impending birth.

Baby crying. A baby is in distress.

Baby far away. The distance determines how near in the future the birth may occur, or how far in the past it had occurred.

Baby appears on right side of a person. Right side indicates the paternal side of family, or the baby is with the father.

Baby appears on left side of a person. Left side is the maternal side of family, or the baby is with the mother.

Empty baby carriage. No baby.

Marriage or Wealth

A ring on the left hand means marriage, or is already married.

A ring being taken off the hand means a possible end to the marriage.

A finger with no ring indicate no marriage or is a single person.

Injury by a ring on the marriage finger indicates an injury or a heartache by a spouse or lover.

A ring that appears far away. The distance the ring appears determines the length of time before the marriage or love will occur.

Fairy princess wedding. A warning that the marriage is make-believe.

Iron bars combined with wedding images. The marriage is confining. A spouse is holding the mate too tightly. The darker and blacker the bars, the more negative the situation.

Large rings or jewelry indicate wealth. The larger the rings or jewelry, the wealthier the person or situation.

Many rings or jewelry indicates wealth from many different sources.

Money

Coins indicate a small amount of money.

Paper currency or dollar bills indicate a larger amount of money.

Piles of money indicate great wealth.

Money or coins falling from an umbrella. There is money for a rainy day. The larger the currency or number of coins determines the amount of money saved or available for future use.

Purse with no money. May lose money or does not have any money.

Cross or Crucifix

Cemetery cross seen on the left. Death on the maternal side of family.

Cemetery cross on right. Death on the paternal side of family.

Cemetery cross in the distance and on left. A future death. The farther away the cross appears, the longer time before the death may occur. ***Do not predict a death unless you are sure this death can be prevented by revealing the incident.***

Cemetery cross in distance on right. A death has already occurred. The farther away the cross appears will determine how long ago the death had occurred.

Small cemetery cross indicates the death of an infant or a child.

White cemetery cross means a death by fate.

Pink roses on cross indicates the death of a loved one.

Spiritual

An image of God may be a spiritual blessing or a positive situation.

An angel indicates a blessing or one is being spiritually protected.

Angels blowing a trumpet. An angel will give a message. The heralding of a spiritual occurrence.

Trumpet. A message. Listen for a message from beyond.

White light. Positive energy. Protection. Good situation.

Rainbow indicates a future success.

Many stars in the sky predict a positive event will occur by fate.

Spiritual umbrella means one is being protected.

Travel

Airplane in flight. Have or will travel.

Airplane unable to fly. The travel is postponed or a delay in plans.

Airplane accident. Warning not to travel or change travel plans.

Pleasure boat. Pleasant trip.

Fast race boat. Will travel fast. A warning not to speed.

Paddling an old or useless boat. A trip will be difficult or uneventful.

Boat on stormy ocean. A warning of trouble. One is confined to a turbulent situation.

Sailboat indicates clear sailing.

Automobile accident. A warning of an accident. Danger in traveling.

Car speeding. A warning not to go too fast. An out of control situation.

Warnings

Dark clouds indicate a warning of trouble. The distance, darkness, and size of the clouds determines the distance and size of the problem.

Storm clouds are far away. Trouble in future, depending upon how far away the clouds appear.

Storm clouds overhead indicate immediate trouble or problems.

Many large storm clouds approaching fast. Much trouble is approaching quickly.

Many large storm clouds slowly approaching. Much trouble is approaching slowly.

Tornado is a warning of a brief, but hard-hitting situation.

Tornado passes overhead. The trouble will not touch or harm you. The trouble will pass by.

Tornado touches near or on you. Will be touched by trouble.

Darkness indicates a dismal situation. Or, one cannot see where to go.

Dark road indicates the way obstructed by the inability to see clearly.

Wind lashing at umbrella indicates trying to protect one's self.

Bells

Bells indicate a change of events.

Wedding bells ringing. Marriage.

Holiday bells indicate a season or happiness on a specific holiday.

Black funeral bells ringing indicate mourning or a possible death. **Do not predict a death.**

Messages

White telephone indicates a happy message or good news.

Black telephone indicates a disappointing message or bad news.

A trumpet indicates that someone is trying to tell you something.

A hand reaching out is an offer to help.

Food

Eating a specific food may be an encouraged to eat specific food.

Spitting out food is a warning not to eat a specific food.

Flowers

Flowers. A pleasant situation. Type of flower may determine the season an event will take place.

Leaves blowing in the wind. Restless. No direction in life. Feels helpless in a situation.

Pink flowers or roses. Love from a deceased. Love from someone.

Four-leaf clover indicates good luck.

Closing Psychometry

The reader may see a curtain closing. This indicates the reading should end and no more information will come through.

A doorknob with an X over it is a warning not to probe into another person's affairs.

The flame of a candle being diminished may indicate it is time to end the reading.

Group Discussion Checklist

What symbols seem natural to you?

What symbols have you already used in other matters?

What symbols will you or have you used?

Share your knowledge of symbols.

Chapter 5
RELEASING FEAR AND ADVANCED PSYCHOMETRY

You have lived through many experiences during this present lifetime. Some have been happy, peaceful times, some unfortunate or fearful. It's also possible you have had several traumatic or misunderstood childhood experiences. Even though you don't consciously remember those experiences, they may remain hidden deep in the subconscious. Those traumatic experiences could affect your present life in different ways, including fears, phobias, allergies, or resentments. Through the process of meditation, you will learn to bring forward a traumatic memory, face the fear within that memory, and recognize why and how that specific fear came to be. Most importantly, you will be able to release the fear. You are not forgetting the memory. You are releasing the fear within that memory. Memories are a way of learning. We don't want to forget them. We want to understand them. The very fact that you are able to face a fear lessens that fear. Just as in a dream, facing the monster within the dream lessens the dreamer's fear.

Each meditation could bring forward a different memory. And within each memory, you may partially or completely release a specific fear. After releasing a fear, you should feel an inner peace on a conscious level and feel more confident and physically healthier. Stress depletes the physical body of energy and decreases one's natural energy and immunity. To release stress and increase energy, meditate often until your fears are no longer threats. They are past. They are done.

Preparing a Personal List

In order to document your progress, you should prepare a personal list. Provide a separate page for each category. Title and date the top of each page, followed by a list of your own issues. You may add to your list at any time. Be sure to date each new issue as it is added. The beginning date will play an important part in confirming your progress. This is your own personal list. You need not share your list with anyone, unless you wish to do so.

Page one is titled "Fears." Write all your fears as they relate to you on this day. A fear may be of an animal, darkness, being alone, being poor, death, heaven, or hell. You may list a specific phobia, fear of a situation, or a person who presents a problem in your present life. You might have no idea where a specific fear originated, but you want it resolved. Write the greatest fear first, followed by the lesser fears. Write any number of fears. Some people may have as few as five or ten fears, while others might have more than fifty. Be honest with your evaluation. Include all fears, because even a lesser fear might cause more conflict than you now understand.

Page two is titled "Dislikes." Your list may contain disliking a certain person, a specific culture, an organization, or a location. List even those things you dislike without justification but wonder why you dislike them. If there is a person you dislike, write the name of that person and the reason you dislike that person. In time, you will understand why it was important to specify the name. You may discover your dislike may have been a misunderstanding of that person, an envy, or a resentment resulting from a past-life experience. After several meditations, your spiritual awareness will open your heart to compassion and understanding, and each resentment may be understood, forgiven, and released with a deeper understanding of its truth. List the greatest dislike first, followed by the lesser ones.

Page three is titled "Beliefs." Write a belief that causes doubt, disharmony, or apprehension in your present life. It may be a medical, political, religious, or economic issue you question or doubt. It may be a church rule or religious doctrine you question, whether it's your religion or another person's religion. Do you fear a specific illness? Do you question if hell exists? Is there life after death? Does God want penance? List any childhood beliefs you were taught or have committed to memory as a fear factor, then think about whether or not each item is true. It could be an old wives' tale you believe is true and wonder if it's harmful. It may be a fear-based belief you simply wonder about or need to clarify in your own mind. Write the most misunderstood or mysterious issues first, ending with those you merely question. Be sure to write even those things you wonder about. Those subconscious uncertainties may be very important and could be affecting your present life.

Page four is titled "Unanswered Questions." How do I deal with physical discord, or how do I find direction in this life? What must I learn from this lifetime? Why am I here? How do I earn my way to heaven? What is cause and effect? What happens after physical death? You have the power and the right to be at peace within your mind and to center that which is divided in thought. Each time you clarify another question, you will be working through your higher self, nullifying another doubt.

Page five is titled "Pleasant Memories." These memories are not intended to release fear but have value as reinforcements to positive thinking. Write any number of pleasant childhood memories you wish to recall and/or clarify. With each meditation, you may revisit a wide range of comforting, tender moments. It doesn't matter how young you were or how long ago the experience took place. Those memories are still embedded in your super-subconscious. Your list may include a specific holiday or childhood birthday you wish to revisit. Do you remember playing with a special friend and want to know why you were so close to that friend? Could she/he have been someone you knew and trusted in a past life? Perhaps you remember being an infant in your mother's arms and want to experience your mother's thoughts at that time. What were your thoughts as an infant? Did you really know your mother or father? By recalling those memories, you may awaken an awareness of why and how you approach certain matters in your daily life. Some memories may reinforce your confidence and security in this present lifetime. Emotional growth is spiritual growth.

Review your list periodically. Each time, you may find several issues have lessened or can be crossed off the list. Be sure to date each issue as it is removed. Or if it has lessened, state to what degree it has diminished. Record all information, even if some details seem inconsequential at the time. In time, the information may reveal a clearer understanding of how an issue had restricted your present thoughts and daily life. Each time you cross an issue off your list, the date will verify how long it took to get positive results. Hopefully, you will have gained an inner peace regarding that issue.

Group Discussion Checklist

Did you prepare a personal list at home?

Did you close your eyes and search your memory for questions to enter in your personal list?

Releasing Fear with Prayer

Prayer is another way to lessen or release fear. Prayer creates a positive energy that works on a deeper level and alters the chemical balance in the physical body. All thoughts have vibratory energy. The positive energy of a prayer influences thoughts and thus affects emotions, which in turn increases physical energy and health. The following prayer may be recited aloud or mentally communicated. Or the group may create its own prayer or change the prayer by asking to be released from a specific fear.

Suggested Prayer

"I release my fears to the God light. I replace my fears with enlightenment. I release all my false beliefs. I no longer believe what I have been told by others. I believe my own truths. I believe what is in my heart. I am enlightened by the God consciousness. Thank you, God, for releasing my fears."

An alternative prayer might simply be: "I release all my fear of _____ to the God light."

Life Paths

We all walk different paths in this present lifetime. As you grow spiritually, you will begin to understand another person's life path is different than your life path. You should not involve yourself in another person's drama. It's his or her lesson, not yours. Remember, you can't go to school for someone else. Through your spiritual enlightenment and checklist discussions, you will become aware of different life issues. You will come to realize people must face their own issues and learn from their own experiences. Don't play a game by living another person's drama.

Meditation

Each meditation is slightly different and progressively increases in complexity. You have already learned to see within the mind's eye, and now you are ready to be challenged even further. "Meditation with Visual Images to Release Fear" is designed to coax the mind to mentally create visual images to be used as psychic tools. These images will be used to release fear. While in meditation, you will be guided to slow your brain waves by counting back from ten to one while visualizing each number. The purpose of focusing on numbers is to retain mental concentration and prevent the mind from wandering off onto trivial matters of the day.

During this meditation, you will be asked to create a special place in your mind's eye where you will do your psychic work. It may be imagined as within a room, on a lawn, or at a special location. It should be a place that represents your idea of peace and contentment. Through mental concentration, you will imagine yourself sitting in a comfortable chair in your special place.

The meditation will guide you to visualize a clock, a calendar, and a screen. Through mental command, you will instruct the clock to move forward or backward in time. You will control the movement of time. You will also be instructed to create a calendar you can mentally move forward or backward in time. When you become familiar with moving time, you will, upon mental command, be able to return to a specific event in your past or present life. As you visualize the calendar's pages flipping over, you will be prompted to visualize a change of seasons. Each season will include color, movement, imagery, and emotion. The vibrant colors and animated scenery are intended to strengthen visualization. Each scene will include movement, which will train the mind to retain focus for longer periods of time. A screen will be imagined in your mind's eye. The screen may be as large as a wall or as small as a book. This screen will, upon mental command, project images, scenery, or anything you request. You may change the scene by the mere action of a thought.

You will be prompted with words to imagine a door in which your angels or guides will appear when called upon. On the first few tries, you might not see your guides or angels. Or the images may appear blurred and without form. Be patient. Don't allow yourself to become negative just because you don't see them immediately. Negativity creates a dull energy field around the physical body that will block your ability to see or sense clearly.

With practice, angels and/or guides may be seen or sensed in full form as shadow of lights, clouds, or transparent figures. They may appear enormous, sometimes larger than a towering building. An angel may appear in fragmented pieces, such as parts of glowing wings or a glistening halo. Expect to see them! Direct a loving thought as you call upon them. With practice, their presence will become unclouded, and their images will become more distinct.

A clairvoyant may see the angels clearly within the mind's eye. A clairsentient may sense them but not see the images. A clairaudient may acknowledge or hear the messages. Some may simply know angels are present but not understand how they are accessing the information. Angels bring with them a feeling of compassion, love, and a feeling of fullness within the room. Be sure to mentally acknowledge the angels' presence, bless them, and thank them for coming.

Angels and guides are always nearby. They are present even before you call upon them. They may influence your daily life more than you realize. Call upon them. They will be there with love in their hearts, even though they have not yet made their presence known to you. Angels are an essence of pure love and compassion. It's your divine right to share your joyous moments or heartaches with them. It may seem the angels haven't answered your prayers as you had requested. Don't be disappointed. What you asked for might not have been in your soul's best interest for spiritual development. When asking for spiritual guidance, ask for "the best for all concerned" so that you will receive the best without interfering in anyone's karmic life pattern.

When guides assist, it's their opportunity to learn, and by sharing their knowledge, they attain a higher spiritual plane of existence. The following comment was said by a guide: "If I learn, then I have not learned anything. But if *we* learn, and I am a part of *we*, then we have learned."

Group Discussion Checklist
What is the guide saying? Explain.

Meditation with Visual Images to Release Fear may be done sitting up or lying down. Sitting is most commonly used when doing a psychic reading or psychometry. Therefore, the first few meditations should be done in a sitting position while training the mind to concentrate.

However, later, when the group feels more comfortable with meditating, they may go into meditation lying down. The more relaxed the body, the deeper the meditation. At the deeper level of concentration, it's possible to reach back and experience an early childhood memory or a past-life event. Each position will accomplish a different result. Both ways will prove beneficial.

Through meditation, you will be prompted to use your mind's eye to visualize traveling back in time to recall a childhood memory. As you mentally project yourself back in time, you may bring forward a fear or phobia that is hidden in your subconscious mind.

As an example, an early childhood incident, such as being stung by a bee while smelling a rose, may not trigger a fear of bees but a fear of the rose upon which the bee sat. That, in turn, may cause an allergic reaction to rose pollen. Through regression, the mind can revisit that memory, recognize the cause, and then release the truth of the experience, which may also release part or all of the allergic reaction to rose pollen.

Meditation with Visual Images to Release Fear will reveal exciting and unusual life experiences you might have forgotten. Expect to visit unknown childhood memories. And while experiencing each memory, mentally request your guides and angels explain the deeper meaning and the value of each experience.

Meditation with Visual Images to Release Fear

"Close your eyes. Visualize a cloud of white light surrounding your body. God is light. God is love. Breathing in the God light. (Pause.) Your forehead is relaxing. Your eyes are relaxing. Slowly take a deep breath and hold it as long as is comfortable. As you exhale, your jaw is relaxing. Your neck is relaxing. (Pause.) Feel the relaxation going down your shoulders. Down your arms. Your hands are relaxing.

"Slowly take a deep breath and hold it as long as is comfortable. As you exhale, your chest is relaxing. Breathing slowly … deeply. Feel the relaxation going down your body … relaxing … relaxing … relaxing. Your thighs are relaxing. Your legs are relaxing. Your feet are relaxing. Concentrate on your third eye. Your forehead is relaxing … relaxing. Your eyes are relaxing … relaxing … relaxing. Becoming pure mind. Knowing exactly where you are at all times. Knowing exactly what you're doing.

"You're looking down a flight of stairs. On each step is a number. The top step is number ten. At the bottom of the stairs is a brilliant light. Feeling very ... very ... peaceful as you slowly float down each step. Going down, ten ... nine ... eight ... seven ... six ... five ... four ... three ... two ... one. Going deeper ... and deeper ... in awareness. Becoming pure mind.

"You're at the bottom of the stairs. In front of you is a doorway. You enter your special place. You're feeling very comfortable. Very safe. You sit down on your comfortable chair. To your left is a clock and calendar. Notice the time on the clock. (Pause.) You have the power to mentally move the clock forward or backward in time. Use your mind to move the hand on the clock forward. (Pause.) Notice the time. Move the hand on the clock back to the current time.

"Look at the calendar. Notice the month. Turn the page to the next month. (Pause.) Turn the pages forward to the next year. You have the power to change time, to go forward or backward in time. Turn the pages back to the present month.

"In front of you is a screen. You have the power to see anything on this screen. This is your picture into another time, another place. On the arm of the chair, you see several small buttons. You may use those buttons to make anything or anyone appear on the screen. Push a button to request loved ones to appear on the screen. (Pause.) Mentally communicate with them. (Pause for a full minute or as long as has been agreed upon.) Bless them. Wrap them in white light. See them fade into the God light. You may mentally communicate with anyone at any time in the past or in the present.

"To your right a door is slowly opening. You see several glowing images floating through the door. (Pause.) Mentally ask, "Are you my guides?" Wait until they have nodded their heads yes or no. (Pause.) They drift closer. (Pause.) Mentally bless them. Thank them for coming. (Pause.) Mentally ask a question. (Wait several minutes or as long as agreed upon.) Thank them for their protection, guidance, and information. They are moving to your side. Feel the love and peace they send you. Feeling very peaceful. Relaxing into your favorite chair. Knowing exactly where you are at all times. Knowing exactly what you are doing.

Concentrate on the calendar. You're drifting deeper ... and deeper ... into awareness. Becoming pure mind.

"It's January. You see a beautiful snow-covered forest. You are drifting into the forest. Snowflakes flutter softly to the ground. A cold wind nudges the bare branches of the tall trees. Reach out with your ethereal hand and touch the snowflakes. (Pause.) Going forward in time.

"It's February. The ground is covered with beautiful white snow. Ahead of you is a snow-covered pond. The pale sun is setting. A golden glow appears as the sun is setting behind the trees. It's growing darker. The sun has set. It's nighttime. Falling snowflakes sparkle in the moonlight. Enjoy the silence of the night. (Pause.) Going forward in time.

"It's March. Rain glistens in the pale morning sun. A gentle wind sweeps across the frozen ground. The rain is softening the frozen pond. (Pause.) Going forward in time.

"It's April. Small blades of grass are poking through the ground. Pale green buds are beginning to open on the maple trees. A gentle morning rain brushes against your face. Feel the coolness of the rain. Smell the freshness of spring. Breathe in the start of a new season. (Pause.) Going forward in time.

"It's May. The earth has come alive with flowering bushes and trees in full bloom. Listen to the sound of birds chirping. Two ducks have landed on the pond. Watch the ducks as they float lazily on the sparkling pond. (Pause.) Going forward in time.

"It's June. Feel the warmth of the morning sun. To your left, purple heather covers the ground as far as the eye can see. Notice the vibrant color. Breathe in the sweet scent of heather. To your right are clusters of tulips. You're drifting toward the tulips. Notice the brilliant yellow color. You reach down and touch the tulips. Feel the smooth, satiny petals. Thank God for the beauty of the earth. (Pause.) Moving forward in time.

"It's July. The morning sun sparkles across the pond. A trail of small ducklings follows a mother duck across the pond. The male duck trails close behind. He moves from side to side, watching the small ducklings. Enjoy. (Wait one minute or more.) Going forward in time.

"It's August. A brilliant sun warms the earth. Feel the warmth of the sun. Breathe in the energy of the sunlight. The ducklings flap their small wings as they race back and forth across the water. (Pause.) Moving forward in time.

"It's September. The leaves on the maple trees have turned brilliant red. The ducklings have grown larger. They're floating across the pond. A cool breeze ripples across the water. Going forward in time.

"It's October. The leaves on the maple trees have turned gold and brown. A cool breeze rustles through the maple trees. Crisp brown leaves flutter down into the pond and bob lazily upon the water. A strong gust of wind ripples across the pond. Feel the autumn chill as the breeze touches your face. The ducklings have grown full size. They turn their face to the wind ... flap their wings as they lift gracefully out of the water. Soaring up ... up ... into the clouds. (Pause.) Going forward in time.

"It's November. An icy wind blows across the frozen ground. A cold mist shrouds the gray, barren trees. In the sky, gray autumn clouds are gathering. Snowflakes are falling, covering the ground and trees. (Pause.) Going forward in time.

"It's December. The sun has set. Darkness is setting in. In the distance, you see a small, snow-covered cottage. You drift closer. You look in the window. The room is lit with colorful lights. People are milling about the room. The smell of freshly baked pie brings back pleasant memories. You are drifting back in time. Drifting back ... back ... back ... in time. You feel your angels lifting you back, back ... in time.

"Mentally ask your guides to show you an important event when you were a child. You see yourself when you're very young ... very small. (Wait ten to twenty minutes or as agreed upon.) Mentally ask your guides to explain why this had happened. (Wait several minutes.) Mentally ask your guides, 'How can I benefit from this experience?' Listen to the words they say to you. (Wait several minutes or as agreed upon.)

"Coming back to the present time. Your breathing is getting deeper ... stronger. Coming back. You will remember the experience and the lessons learned. Knowing exactly where you are at all times. Knowing exactly what you're doing. Coming back. Your breathing is getting deeper ... stronger. Slowly take a deep breath. Coming back. On the count of three, you will open your eyes, feeling very, very good. Coming back. One. Every day in every way, I'm getting better and better. (Pause.) Two. Every day in every way, I'm getting better and better. (Pause.) Feeling very, very good. Three. Open your eyes."

*End of meditation.

A discussion of the checklist is an important part of each lesson. The group is encouraged to share their experiences if they're not of a personal nature. Examine what each has learned and of what value it has taught them. After this meditation, each person may have released several issues, and it may happen without any effort on his or her part. Often, it's just a matter of listening to another person's experience that releases a specific fear or anxiety.

Group Discussion Checklist

Did you visualize the clock, calendar, and screen?

Did you see guides or angels coming through the door?

Did you visualize or sense the change of seasons?

Did you feel the cold, sun, wind, or breeze?

Did you arrive at a childhood memory?

Did your guides take you? Or did you go to the childhood memory by drifting back in time?

What experience did you examine?

What, if anything, did you learn from that experience?

What, if any, misunderstanding did you clear up in your mind?

How might uncovering a specific childhood experience help you in this present life?

Did you experience a spiritual encounter?

Check Your Personal List

It's time to check your personal list in the privacy of your own home. You may not realize the progress you've made, but after using Meditation with Visual Images to Release Fear, you may find your spiritual awareness will have heightened and you have changed your mind about what you had previously believed. Your personal list will be a confirmation of when, why, how, and to what degree each fear or issue has been diminished or released. For instance, you now understand why you had disliked or felt uncomfortable about a specific person. You now believe you might have misinterpreted that person's actions. Perhaps what you thought was laziness was really ill health. Maybe a person's crude or coarse language was really due to low self-esteem or lack of education. You have come to realize what you had believed was a deliberate action was really quite unintentional.

It's important to record what you now understand about a specific fear or issue. Each issue may have many facets or undisclosed causes and might be further enlightened in the next meditation. Sometimes facing a fearful memory will bring closure to several other fears. In time, you will notice some fears have simply disappeared. They no longer exist in your present life.

Advanced Psychometry

Now that you have learned to use the images, a clock, calendar, and screen, you will find your psychometry will greatly improve. Use your intuition to select a partner for a psychometry reading. Select a person of whom you have little or no knowledge. A stranger will present less chance to influence your reading with logic. There should be no ego. There are no set rules. This is not a test to see who is best. It's a way to become familiar with your personal guides, feel and sense their presence, and develop your psychic ability.

A female may find psychometry easier than a male does. There are many reasons for this. One reason is Western society encourages females to grow in awareness and sensitivity. A mother raising a child has the opportunity to create a natural sensitivity. When a baby is young, the mother finds herself sleeping with one ear listening. The scientific term for this level of light rest is alpha level. She is relaxed at this level but aware. Although she doesn't know it, she is training herself to lower her brain waves enough to get a good night's sleep yet remain alert enough to focus her attention quickly if the baby cries. She is learning to be sensitive and aware, even though she is asleep.

As the baby grows, the mother becomes aware of the baby's changing actions, expressions, and moods. This creates an added sensitivity, the ability to use her intuition. The mother also becomes sensitive to changes in her baby's tone of voice. Soon, she can tell the difference between a cry of anger or discontentment and a desperate cry for help. The woman continues to train herself to sense changes in sound and feeling.

Because the male is physically stronger than the female, society expects him to be more aggressive. He has been encouraged to become more physical at the expense of his gentler, more sensitive side. A generation or two ago, men would spend their day in the workforce. Their demands required a completely different kind of attention. They didn't have the luxury of quieting down to study one issue at a time.

When the man came home, he expected to rest after a full day at work. So, in the past, the average man had trained his mind to turn off disturbing sounds during sleep. He would drop to a level of deep sleep known as theta, and he was unaware of everything around him. He had unknowingly turned off his ability to sense things as easily as his wife does. He had little opportunity to train his mind to drift between alpha and theta levels on command.

Fortunately, there is a change taking place in the way society views the sexes. Now there is more encouragement given for men to develop their sensitivity. Hopefully, there will soon be a balance of sensitive men standing beside sensitive women.

The group should read the following suggestions before beginning psychometry. They are not listed in any specific order. The reader will use only those suggestions as they apply to the present reading.

The reader may do any or all of the following:

- Concentrate on the forehead, the mind's eye.
- Visualize a screen, clock, and calendar.
- Wait until he or she sees a year or date appear on the calendar.
- Describe what he or she is seeing (i.e., the person, clothing, country, nationality, year, scenery, and each emotion).
- Mentally ask the image questions.
- Mentally suggest the image answer by moving its head from side to side for no or up and down for yes.
- Mention if the scene appears in color. The more vivid the color, the more important the scene.
- Go back to a childhood experience to probe the reasons for an allergy, fear, habit, phobia, etc.
- Go backward in time several months or years until an important event presents itself.
- Rise above a tragic scene. A reader should not become emotionally involved. Release an emotion by mentally saying; "I am rising above the scene. I feel no emotion with the scene. I am only observing."
- Stop the meditation if he/she feels it's best not to continue. It may be a suggestion from the guides.
- Do not allow observers to interfere by asking questions. Only the partner (client) receiving the reading should ask a question. An outside voice may interrupt the reading.

- Do not allow ego to enter the reading. Ego will interfere with or deplete the energy of a reading.
- Hold his or her hand up to stop the partner from asking too many questions.
- Do not make any false description or report.
- Do not speak too loudly, as it may distract others.
- Discuss the reading in a whisper when it is done.

The client receiving the reading may do any or all of the following:

- Be patient while the reader waits for images, symbols, or scenery to appear in the mind's eye before asking a question.
- Give the reader plenty of time to relate what he/she is sensing or seeing.
- Confirm an identifiable name or place as a direct hit to encourage the reader.
- Take notes to be reviewed at a later time.
- Ask only one question at a time.
- Do not ask a compound question that requires mixed answers.
- Wait until the reader has explained what he/she is seeing before asking another question.
- Do not interrupt the reader with too many questions.
- Direct the reader to go back in time to a specific holiday, occasion, or date in time.
- Assist the reader by softly directing, "Going back in time. Back … back … back in time."
- Ask a specific question, such as, "Why is (your name) fearful of (name a person, place, animal, or phobia)?"
- If a death scene or a traumatic incident occurs, the client may assist the reader by softly suggesting any of the following phrases:
  - "You are rising above the scene."
  - "You are only witnessing the scene."
  - "You do not feel any emotion or pain."
  - "You are only observing."

Listen attentively to each reader to learn new techniques and methods. Eventually, each reader will acquire his or her own method, one that works best for him/her. However, even that method will change as the members develop spiritually.

Exercise. Advanced Psychometry

Sit up straight. Don't cross the legs. Close the eyes and take a deep breath. Slowly release the breath to slow down the brain waves. Mentally place protection around you, such as God light or white light. Mentally ask your angels or personal guides to assist.

Two people will sit facing each other. You will be the reader. The other person is the client. You will hold an object that belongs to the client. It may be a ring, watch, or any personal article. You will move the object through your hands. Use the fingertips to feel the object. Allow the vibrations to form images in your mind's eye. Verbally express what you are seeing, feeling, or sensing. Start talking.

Your eyes may display a rapid eye movement (REM) or a fluttering under the eyelids. This usually occurs when, you, the reader, is seeing or sensing an experience within the mind's eye. During REM, the client may encourage you, the reader, by asking a question. "What do you see?" Or, "Can you explain what you are seeing?"

The first few tries at psychometry will usually present current affairs. Images of the client's daily events may just pop into your thoughts or mind's eye.

Exercise. Select a new partner. Begin psychometry reading.

Group Discussion Checklist
What, if any, images did you see?
Did the images become clearer as you spoke?
Did you have a direct hit? A direct hit is a personal message or one that applies only to the client. Identifiable names and places would be considered direct hits.
Did the object feel hot or cold?
Which hand did you hold the object in? Did you try the other hand as well?
Is it easier to read for one person as opposed to another?

Do you understand why it is easier to read one person rather than another person? If so, explain.

Chapter 6

THOUGHT FORMS AND TELEPATHICALLY DIRECTED THOUGHTS

Is it possible for other people to feel our thoughts? Do they know or sense what we think about them? It's often said, "Thoughts are things occupying a place in space." What is a *thing*? For that matter, what is a *thought*? We know when something has occurred by the result of its action. We can't see electricity, but we know it exists by the current used to operate lights, computers, and televisions. We can't see our thoughts, but we know they exist because our mind is full of thoughts every day of our lives. Does a thought just stay in our head until it's released by its own action or until another thought takes over? Or can it leave our mind and enter the mind of another?

"Meditation to Telepathically Direct Thoughts" will introduce the use of mental telepathy, awaken your sixth sense as means of communication, and offer techniques to manipulate the ethereal hands and body. This chapter is intended to increase the power of your mind. The exercise will increase your ability to use your mind to create thought energy that will allow you to move a person toward you or away from you. Life is often filled with situations where you wish you were able to remove a person from your space. Meditation to Telepathically Direct Thoughts will do just that.

Thoughts travel instantaneously through the atmosphere by way of mental telepathy. They can be experienced physically and metaphysically.

The person receiving a subtle thought may sense it as a slight impression. Sincere thoughts, as in prayer, can have a peaceful or calming effect upon the person who is praying. Even the person receiving the prayer, no matter how far away, may feel a portion of its calming effect, whether he/she is aware of the prayer or not. Collective thoughts, such as thousands of people praying to safeguard our country, have a cumulative energy and can empower an area with positive energy.

A single thought is very powerful. As an example, a woman glances across the room at a man, smiles, and sends a thought of passionate interest. Because her thought was sincerely sent, it acted as a vibratory energy. The man may not consciously have known he received the thought, but the energy of it altered his emotions, causing his aura to glow. He intuitively turns toward her. He has taken notice. On the other hand, if she had sent a thought of *I don't like you,* that thought would have transmitted a dull, negative vibration. The man might react to the subtle hint of negative energy. He would be *turned off.* He would turn away. Thoughts are sent and received in different degrees. They will affect their target more intensely when directed with ardent love or extreme anger. Therefore, we know a thought exists by its affect upon others.

Group Discussion Checklist
    Can you feel negative vibrations when they are directed at you?
    Have you ever sensed or felt when someone really cares about you?
    Have you felt "turned on" by someone's thoughts toward you?
    How can you use this natural intelligence for your benefit?
    What other ways can you use the power of your mind?

Thought Patterns
    In the beginning, people were born with the natural ability of sensing. Prehistoric men didn't use a large vocabulary to communicate their ideas. They used their natural intelligence—extra sensory perception. However, as time passed, this natural ability has been replaced it with a verbal, less spiritual means of communication. Sincerity and compassion for others have lessened because egocentric people no longer used their inner sensitivity toward the feelings and needs of others. Today, not all people think with compassion as God had intended.

Consider the vast number of personal thoughts transmitted into the universe daily. Thoughts rush out into the atmosphere, interacting with everything and everyone. Each person's thoughts create millions of positive or negative vibrations. Thoughts are a communication between all people and in all people. Everyone is connected by thoughts, even if they don't realize they are sending or receiving a thought.

If a thought could be seen, it would appear as vibrating particles of energy with flashes of dazzling colors moving at a great rate of speed. Thoughts can be and have been created by an individual or by mass consciousness. Thoughts can be of love or fear, wants or needs, likes or dislikes, adoration or prejudices; the list goes on and on. Thoughts from the past can remain in the atmosphere for long periods of time. Thoughts that stir the imagination of successful inventors are often received in the still of the night or while nearly asleep. Thoughts still affect the present and can affect the future.

Natural Protection

Most homes are blessed with a natural protection that has been created by the positive white aura energy of the homeowner. However, a homeowner can unwittingly change the vibrations of a loving home to a place of agitation by his or her own thoughts. Like draws like. If a homeowner constantly dwells on negative or irritating thoughts, that energy can accumulate. If the negative thoughts continue over a long period, it can cause a spiraling vortex. This may cause a hole or break in the natural white-light protection.

Spirits see vibrating energy, whether it is light or dark, positive or negative. When an undesirable spirit sees a vortex of dark energy spiraling from a house, it may be drawn to feed upon that negative energy. It can enter the room or house through the vortex opening. If that spirit remains in the house for weeks or months, it will begin to project its own negative energy, thereby intensifying the dismal feeling within the house. Negative spirits find reassurance in like-minded negative energy. If people realized the full impact of their thoughts, I'm sure they would choose their thoughts more carefully.

Group Discussion Checklist

Do you feel uncomfortable in a negative person's home?

Do you sense a person's home is negative long before you enter it?

Will you now consider how your thoughts can affect your entire household?

The Effect of a Thought

Irritating thoughts directed toward a person can be felt as an uncomfortable, edgy feeling. When a person is constantly irritated, energy can accumulate until it leaves a tense, jittery feeling within the room. Tension is easily recognized by an animal, especially a dog or cat, which reacts to the irritation with apprehension, shuddering, or suspicion.

Depressive thoughts have the power to drain one's energy much like a vampire sucking one's life force. A depressed person is constantly discharging large amounts of negative energy similar to a gray aura. This energy can accumulate within a room, a house, or an area. If the depression continues over long periods, those gray vibrations may gather enough energy to form a slow-moving, gray ball of energy. This vibratory energy swirls around and around and can grow as large as seven or eight feet in diameter, leaving a heavy, gloomy atmosphere within the room. Swirling gray energy cannot be seen with the naked eye but can be seen or sensed by psychics. Most animals will react to the depressive feeling with a lethargic attitude or sadness. Depressive thoughts have the power to drain the positive energy of anyone who enters that house and could adversely affect the average person, whether they are psychic or not.

Violent thoughts sent with intense anger create a faster-moving, erratic vibration. When a violent thought is directed toward a person, it will cause that person to feel edgy, fearful, or tense. Such distress can drain a person of his or her natural energy. When violent thoughts continue over a long period of time, that energy can accumulate within the room. The constant bombardment of violent thoughts within a confined area can eventually generate into a fast, swirling motion. If the violence escalates, it causes the vibrations to swirl faster and faster, gathering more momentum until it creates a spiraling vortex within the room similar to an invisible cyclone. If the swirling vibrations are strong enough, they can break through the home's natural protection, causing an opening in the atmosphere. Like draws like. Violent spirits may be drawn toward the violent energy, and they can enter through the vortex opening. Animals often hesitate or refuse to enter a room where there are violent spirits.

Group Discussion Checklist

Can you recognize irritation in a person's eyes, face, or body language? Explain.

Have you ever or can you feel a person's irritation before they enter the room?

If confined with a depressed person for a long period, do you feel drained? Explain.

Have you recognized an animal's sensitivity toward a depressed or angry person? Explain.

How do you recognize violence in a face, eyes, or body language?

When in a violent situation, do you feel a need to remove yourself from the area?

Explain the difference between irritating, depressive, and violent thoughts.

How do you protect yourself from another person's depression?

Have you tried different methods of protection, such as covering yourself with white light or asking your angels for protection?

Do you wrap the God light around you as protection when in a negative situation?

What other method have you used to protect yourself or your home from a negative situation?

Visible Signs of Negativity

A haunted house may manifest different degrees of negative energy. The house may emit a dull, gloomy energy, and it usually gives off an uninviting feeling. The outside of the house may appear unkempt. A house that has negative spirits or negative energy will usually display a dark or dull overcast to the window glass. This dull effect can be the result of many things. It may be caused by the occupant's negative gray aura, his or her buildup of irritating energy. It may be a result of a spirit's fear or anger. Under most circumstances, spirits cannot touch or physically hurt a person; however, they can project thoughts. They can influence a person's state of mind. Ghosts are usually not evil. They simply haven't changed their negative thoughts because they have not yet crossed over into the God light. The best way to prevent undesirable spirits from entering a house is for the homeowner to make a serious effort to change his or her own negative thoughts to positive thoughts of love and compassion toward others.

People who are psychic or naturally sensitive will feel the vibrations of a negative house. Those who are less sensitive and more egocentric will react to the negativity to a lesser degree, but they will react. Neither space nor time can obstruct the energy of a thought form. Only the target's inability to sense can dull its recognition.

Group Discussion Checklist

Have you experienced negative energy? Explain.

Can you recognize from the outside of a house whether the resident is angry or irritated? If so, how?

Have you noticed a different hue to the windows of a haunted house?

Do you reinforce the natural protection of your home by using positive thoughts and compassion toward all others?

Do you surround your home and family with white light?

What other method have you used to reinforce the natural protection of your home?

Thoughts Are Things Occupying a Place in Space

The following story is a true experience. While I was in psychic training, my teacher, June Black, repeatedly emphasized the words, "Thoughts are things occupying a place in space." But no matter how many times she explained this phenomenon in technical terms or tried to impress the importance of a thought, I just couldn't grasp the true meaning until I had experienced it myself.

Imagine a class of students sitting in a circle in a dimly lit room. I was one of those students. I was sitting on the opposite side of the circle across from the teacher. June was teaching hands-on healing. As the class progressed, I noticed June did not look well. Her complexion was pale, and her eyes seemed listless.

A thought crossed my mind, "I hope June goes in the circle for a healing. She seems tired."

At that time, I was not aware my innocent thought had been instantly transmitted outward into the universe as colorful waves of energy. I was also unaware the universe is filled with energy forms such as angels and spiritual beings who can see the vibrant colors of a sincere thought. I was soon to learn how quickly thoughts are acted upon by the universe.

June glanced up curiously. She closed her eyes as the impact of my thought rushed toward her. She felt the thought in a physical way and saw it metaphysically in the form of an angelic, female figure. She directed a question toward me. "Marie, did you just send an angel to do healing on me?"

"No," I answered, unaware my thought had actually been a request.

"Well, did you think of sending an angel to heal me?"

Again, I answered, "No."

"Did you have a thought that I need healing?" she asked.

"Yes, I hoped you would get in the circle for healing."

"I want to thank you," June said. "Your thought was answered. The angelic figure of a beautiful woman drifted across the circle from where you are sitting. She set her hands on me, and I received a healing."

Now I understood the phrase, "Thoughts are things occupying a place in space." I had just learned the person to whom I had directed my thought had been the physical recipient of that thought. I was still a student, and at that time, I didn't realize that each thought reflects a different color and degree of energy, depending upon the intensity or sincerity with which it was sent. Because my thought had been sincerely sent, it had been picked up by the universe at some point midway between my teacher and me. That innocent thought had vibrated at a terrific rate of speed, and the universal energy had received it instantaneously.

Most people might not have understood the angelic figure was the result of a thought. However, June Black, having been active in the field of paranormal study for over forty years in London, England, had learned from her own experience that thoughts are an actual force of energy. Because she was clairvoyant, she was able to see the thought in its physical form.

Group Discussion Checklist

Do you feel the effect if someone is thinking positively or negatively about you? Explain.

Knowing like draws like, what can you expect when you make an effort to direct a positive thought toward another person?

Have you seen a thought in your mind's eye?

Suggest a positive thought to send to a family member or friend.

Do you have a friend of relative who needs healing? If so, suggest a positive thought which can be sent with a healing effect.

Are you aware of the thoughts you are sending into the universe?

Name some thoughts that people send out daily.

Will you now make an effort to think with more compassion and understanding toward others?

How Thoughts Affect the Spirit World

Have you ever wondered if a deceased relative knows what you are thinking? Do you constantly dwell on a negative situation caused by a deceased person? If you were sure the deceased could hear your thoughts, would you change those thoughts?

When a single thought is repeatedly projected outward, it accumulates energy. If many people repeat the same thought with sincerity or judgment, that thought has an accumulative power that can influence the living, the earth, the atmosphere, and the spirit world. Yes, a thought can pierce the veil and reach beyond the physical world. Much like an arrow, a thought can be directed at its target with good or bad intentions.

Spirits feel the effect of a thought when it's specifically projected toward them. They can feel the peaceful energy of a prayer or the negative energy of resentment. They are affected. Just as physical punishment weighs heavy on the physical body, a judgmental thought weight heavy upon a spirit. However, even though most spirits feel the effect of a judgmental thought directed at them, they don't usually take it as a personal offense. They still feel it, but if they have passed over into the God light and are now closer to the God consciousness, they are usually nonjudgmental.

After a person has passed into spirit, it's important that the living make a sincere effort not to be judgmental. Keep your thoughts positive, pure, and peaceful. Do you want to be responsible for misjudging another person's intention? Do you really know what was on his or her mind when he/she committed what you consider an inappropriate thought or act? You don't have to like that decision or agree with his or her actions, but you should try to be compassionate in your understanding.

Group Discussion Checklist

Do you still hold resentment toward a person in the spirit world?

Do you now realize how your resentment weighs heavily upon the deceased?

Do you realize a spirit's life path might have been to experience such an event?

Do you wonder how you would have acted if the same scenario had been presented to you? If so, can you think of a way to forgive that person?

Have you been too judgmental in what might have been a spirit's life lesson to learn?

Have you called upon the angels to help you lose a resentment you still hold toward another?

Test your ability. Close your eyes and call upon an angel for healing on yourself or on another person. Watch within your mind's eye as angels or spirit healers perform.

Check your personal list. Have you released any fears or resentments?

Meditation to Telepathically Direct Thoughts will introduce the use of mental telepathy, awaken the sixth sense as a means of communication, and offer techniques to manipulate the ethereal hands and body. If meditating alone, it would be helpful to make a tape or recording of the following meditation for your personal use at home.

Meditation to Telepathically Direct Thoughts

"Close your eyes. Concentrate on your third eye. A beam of light is coming toward you. It's growing stronger, brighter ... and brighter. This is your God light. God is light. God is love. Slowly take a deep breath, breathing in the God light. Hold it as long as is comfortable. As you exhale, you are feeling very peaceful. Knowing exactly where you are at all times. Knowing exactly what you're doing.

"Slowly take a deep breath and hold it as long as is comfortable. As you slowly exhale, your forehead is relaxing. Your eyes are relaxing ...

relaxing … relaxing. Your neck is relaxing. (Pause.) You're breathing slowly … deeply. Feel the relaxation going down your shoulders … down your arms. Your hands are relaxing. Slowly take a deep breath and hold it as long as is comfortable. As you exhale, your chest is relaxing. Your stomach is relaxing. (Pause.) Your spine is relaxing. Feel each vertebrae relaxing … relaxing … relaxing. Going deeper … and deeper … into awareness. Becoming pure mind. Knowing exactly where you are at all times. Knowing exactly what you're doing.

"Concentrate on the third eye. You see a person coming toward you. With your ethereal hands, reach out and touch that person's clothing. Feel the fabric … the texture. Touch the thread, the stitching. Notice the color. Use the energy of your mind to gently nudge the person to the right. Watch as the person sways to the right. (Pause.) Use your mind to nudge the person to the left. Watch as the person moves to the left. (Pause.) Mentally tell him/her to stand still. Use your mind to hold the person still. (Pause.) Mentally draw the person toward you.

"Mentally bless the person. Watch the aura grow lighter … and brighter … as the blessing surrounds his or her body. (Pause.) Reach out with your ethereal hands. Touch the glowing aura. Move your hands slowly around the aura. Feel the smooth, calming vibration. (Pause.) Change your thoughts. Suggest the person has made a big mistake. Project words of regret for the mistake. (Pause.) Watch the aura grow gray and dull. (Pause.) Sense the sadness. Feel the emotions. (Pause.) Reach out with your ethereal hands and touch the aura. Move your hands around, feeling the dull aura. Notice the rough, sticky feeling. (Pause.) Change your thoughts. Suggest the error has been corrected. The person smiles. Watch the aura begin to glow. The aura is growing brighter … and brighter. Feel the happiness. A smile crosses your face as you join in the happiness. Breathing in the glowing light of the aura. Connect with the person. Listen to the message. (Pause for a minute or as long as has been agreed upon.) Bless the person. Thank the person for coming. See the spirit of the person rise upward until it disappears into the light.

"You're looking up at white clouds. Your body is becoming lighter … lighter … lighter. You're rising up … up … toward the billowy clouds. There is an angel to your right. There is an angel to your left. You are rising … floating upward. Reach out. Use your ethereal hands to guide you. Feel the ease of movement as you glide higher … and higher. Use your ethereal hands to glide in ... and out ... of the clouds. Enjoy. (Pause for a full minute or as long as been agreed upon.) Direct your hands toward a beautiful cloud. You are floating toward the cloud. You settle gently upon the cloud. Feeling very peaceful. Knowing exactly where you are at all times. Knowing exactly what you're doing. You ... are in control.

"The sunlight peeks between the clouds. You glide into the sunlight. Feel the warmth of the sun. Slowly take a deep breath, breathing in the energy of the sunlight. Above you see bands of glowing angels. Feel the unconditional love they send. Breathe in the love and compassion they offer. (Pause.) Mentally thank the angels for guiding you in meditation. See them nod. Listen to their personal message. (Wait several minutes or as long as has been agreed upon.)

"Your breathing is growing stronger ... deeper. On the count of three, you will open your eyes, feeling very, very good. Coming back. Your breathing is getting deeper ... stronger. Coming back. Every day in every way, I'm getting better and better. (Pause.) One. Breathing deeper ... stronger. Two. Every day in every way, I'm getting better and better. (Pause.) Three. Your eyes are open. Feeling very, very good."

*End of meditation.

The preceding meditation was a rehearsal of mentally sending and receiving thoughts. With each thought you directed toward the spirit, you visualized or sensed the aura increasing or decreasing in size and color. You used your mind's eye to see, and your mind to mentally communicate. You also used the power of your mind to move the body from side to side. You were introduced to the use of your ethereal hands and body. The very thought of your ethereal body rising toward the clouds should have given you the pleasant feeling of rising. In addition, you used your ethereal hands to control the movement of your ethereal body. This may be quite new to some members. Most people never thought of manipulating their body or feeling with their ethereal hands. Of course, it's much easier to feel with your ethereal hands or transmit thoughts while in meditation than it is on the physical level. The mind is capable of a deeper concentration when in meditation because it's not distracted by outside activity.

To test your ability to use your ethereal hand, try this. Next time you are among a crowd of people, sitting in church, or waiting in an office, test your ability to mentally communicate with another person. Your eyes don't have to be closed. You can use your mind to mentally reach out with your ethereal hand and gently touch a person on the shoulder. Watch the person move slightly as a response to your touch.

Group Discussion Checklist

While meditating, did you feel your ethereal body rising?

Did you use your ethereal hands to guide you?

Did you feel the lightness and freedom as you traveled among the clouds?

How or what did you feel as you drifted among the clouds?

Did you see or sense the angels?

What, if any, feeling came from the angels?

Did you move the person from side to side with your mind?

Did you sense, feel, or see the person's aura?

How did the light aura feel as opposed to the dull aura?

Did you feel or sense the change of emotion as the aura changed from dark to light?

Suggest other ways to test your mental telepathy.

Preparation for Mental Telepathy

The group should place their chairs in as perfect a circle as possible. A circle is a strong shape, both physically and metaphysically. A circle can retain more energy than squares, rectangles, or triangles because curved surfaces are stronger than straight surfaces. Chairs should be placed evenly to avoid any large gaps or openings. If there is a large space between seats, the person sitting next to the space will mentally request an angel or a guide to fill the space. This will prevent positive energy from escaping and negative energy from entering. No one should sit outside the circle. The powerful God light protection is held within the circle, but its protection decreases outside the circle.

The members will close their eyes and place their hands on their laps, palms up. They will breathe in deeply, mentally drawing the God light in through the top of their heads, direct it into their body, and then send it out their upturned palms toward the center of the circle. Palms should be positioned upward so energy can be directed into the circle. Palms facing down on the lap with the thumb and forefinger held together will retain the energy within that person. Any member who is in need of physical or emotional healing may leave his or her palms facing down until he/she senses the God light has accomplished the silent healing, at which time the palms should intuitively turn upward. The very fact that the light is surging through each member will have a healing effect on physical and metaphysical levels, whether the palms are facing upward or turned down. The God light, white light, or an angelic presence is a delicately sensitive but extremely powerful energy that can be used for healing and protection.

Angels and personal guides of those present also draw in energy. The circle shape will harness the combined energy to increase the group's psychic awareness. This exercise is best performed when ten or more have joined the circle. If it is done with only three or four, the thoughts will be less effectively transmitted. With practice, it will become easier to sense a thought form without the assistance of the circle's energy. Eventually, it will feel natural to use mental communication on a physical and a metaphysical level. The purpose of this exercise is to make it easier for you to sense the slight touch of your angels and guides as they gently nudge or guide you in a safe direction.

A prayer for spiritual guidance and protection may be recited or mentally expressed. Those who are clairvoyant may see bands of angels, white light, or spiritual guides enter through the top of the circle or surround the circle. Those who are clairsentient may feel or sense the angelic compassion and love surrounding the circle. Be patient. Recognition of spiritual guidance will take time, sincerity, and practice.

The following exercise will demonstrate techniques to mentally send, receive, sense, and feel thought forms. The group will use their ethereal hands to telepathically move a physical body with their mind.

Exercise. Telepathy to Move the Physical Body

The group will sit in a circle. Each member will take a slow, deep breath and slowly exhale. This will relax the physical body and slow down the brain waves, making it easier to tune into his or her psychic awareness. Two people will be selected to stand in the center of the circle. One person will be the *sender*. The other is the *receiver*. For this exercise, the sender will be known as he, and the receiver will be known as she. The receiver will stand with her back to the sender. She should not see any movement or know what the sender is about to send.

The sender will announce he is ready to use his mind to push the receiver away. On the first try, the sender will tell which direction he will be directing his energy but not exactly when. The receiver will take a deep breath, slow down her brain waves, and tune into her psychic awareness. The sender is now ready to mentally send a force of energy with his mind.

The sender may try any or all of the following techniques:

- Mentally project a thought of pushing the receiver away.
- Project energy out the hands, forcing the receiver away.
- Imagine or sense powerful vibrations pushing outward.
- Project the thought of the whole body as an energy field pushing the receiver away.
- Mentally suggest words like "go away" or "move away."
- Project an image, such as the wind blowing outward.
- Project any image or symbol intuitively presented.
- Project one thought at a time.

The receiver should not see the sender's hand gestures, or be influenced by any movement or sound. She may keep her eyes open or, from time to time, close her eyes to concentrate within her mind's eye.

The receiver should:

- Stand still in the center of the circle until she feels a need to move.
- Mentally accept or sense the energy being projected.
- Tune into a personal guide and wait for a gentle nudge.
- Allow her body to sway with the movement.
- Look within the third eye to see symbols that direct her body to move in one direction or another.
- Sense which way the energy is pushing her body.

On the second try, the sender will inform the receiver he will now mentally draw the receiver toward him. The sender may:

- Imagine the receiver moving closer.
- Imagine energy drawing the receiver closer.
- Mentally project words such as "come" or "move closer."
- Project images or symbols, such as arrows showing direction.
- Project a feeling of a drawing motion.
- Use any method that intuitively presents itself.

When the receiver has responded to the pull of energy, the sender is now ready for the third unspoken message. On the first two tries, it was necessary to verbally inform the receiver which direction she was to move. This made the expectation of movement anticipated, easier to recognize. The real test is on the third try. The sender will not inform the receiver what he is about to do. He must send only one direction at a time to avoid mixed signals. This is a silent, mental message exercise.

The sender may:

- Use the ethereal hands to move the person forward or backward.
- Mentally draw the person closer or force the person away.
- Imagine thoughts of swaying from side to side.
- Project thoughts of erratic pulses or jerking movements in one direction or another.
- Mentally think the receiver to the left or to the right.
- Turn the receiver around and around by imagining a circular motion.
- Mentally project the words "around and around."
- Not communicate a negative message. Those thoughts might be picked up by the receiver and may be redirected, knowingly or unknowingly, back to you, the sender.
- Not change his or her mind in the middle of a thought.
- Not try to fool the receiver by sending mixed signals.

This is not a test to see who is best. This is your spiritual development and should be done on a sincere, spiritual level. Keep your thoughts clear, positive, and honorable. Remember, these exercises are designed to increase communication with your spiritual guides.

The receiver may:

- Stand with eyes closed or open while receiving the unspoken message.
- Allow her body to move with each gentle vibration sensed or received.
- Mentally call upon guides for spiritual assistance.
- Look within the mind's eye to see which direction to follow.
- Sense which direction she is being sent.
- Allow the body to sway with the flow of energy.

The members will switch places and repeat the exercise until each has experienced sending and receiving thoughts. Because each person is unique, each may develop a different ability. Some will be better at sending, while others will find it easier to receive or sense energy as it approaches. Don't be disappointed if this is not your strong suit. Perhaps a different ability will be awakened by the various exercises to follow. Eventually, you will find your strong point. The rewarding aspect of recognizing thought forms is to strengthen the command of your mind and to develop a deeper awareness of your spiritual guidance.

Begin exercise.

The previous exercise increased your ability to sense guidance from the spirit world. Angels and guides have been sent by God. They are here to encourage you to take the best path for your soul's journey. Each time you connect with your personal guides, you will find it easier to respond to their daily guidance and to sense the path they encourage you to take. It will become easier to recognize their warning of danger, thereby avoiding mistakes or dangerous situations. Also, with practice, you will be better equipped to use your mind to move disruptive people away or draw agreeable people closer. Repeat this exercise often but don't limit yourself to communicating with only your spirit guides. God is your supreme guidance. Call upon Him for guidance, even if it's just for practice. In time, you will sense His unconditional love, and it will awaken the "honor of self" within.

Group Discussion Checklist

Did you use your ethereal hands to move the receiver?
Are you better at sending or receiving?
As the receiver, did you sense the incoming thought?
What words or symbols did you receive intuitively?
Have you ever sensed a thought? If so, how did it affect you?
Did you see or sense your spiritual guidance?
Did you feel your guide nudge or move you in a direction?
Would you recognize gentle guidance if it occurs again?

Chapter 7
HOW TO SENSE A LIAR

Do you know when someone is lying? Can you see it in his or her eyes? Some people avoid eye contact, turn their faces partly away, or look out of the corner of their eyes when lying. Some close their eyes as they lie. They find it difficult to face the person to whom they are lying. Others stare hard, determined to convince you they are not lying. People often respond with a higher pitch in their voice when lying or put their hands in their pockets as a way of hiding the truth. Some people turn their backs or walk away. It is their way of backing away from the truth. These are only a few physical characteristics the average person might display when lying. However, there are more than just physical mannerisms that expose a liar. There are also metaphysical signs. Lies can be detected in the aura.

All people have an energy field or an aura that changes from hour to hour, depending upon the body's physical or emotional condition or the thought it is currently expressing. The aura registers a dull hue when it contains a lie, and a lighter glow when it's confident in its own truth. Thoughts travel through the atmosphere as waves of color vibrations, and they can be received in subtle ways.

A deceptive thought emits a dull gray vibration and can affect those nearby in a negative manner. If, on the other hand, the thought expresses happiness and love, its lightness will raise another person's vibrations in a positive, comforting manner. Maintaining positive thoughts improves one's energy and health, while negative thoughts drain or deplete one's energy. Therefore, it's important to think positive, loving thoughts. Love is energy. Energy is love. Each loving thought contains energy that will empower you to a closer relationship with your God consciousness, your higher self.

Recognizing a lie can be helpful. When you learn to become aware of other people's emotions, you can easily surmise their intentions, thereby avoiding problems in your daily life. You can be vigilant to detach yourself from a negative situation or avoid being drawn into another person's deception. By remaining truthful, you can boost the level of positive energy in others as well as yourself.

Each exercise should begin with a meditation. Any previous meditations may be used to draw energy in and to strengthen one's psychic awareness. Meditation to Telepathically Direct Thoughts is suggested because it deals with sensing and feeling with the ethereal hands. However, the group may suggest another meditation. If most members are novices, seven or more members will be needed to draw enough energy to perform the following exercise. As the group grows larger and the members strengthen their psychic abilities, the energy will increase, and the exercise will be more successful.

Exercise 1. Sense a Liar

The members will divide into groups. Each group will work in a different area of the room. One person from each group will be the detective. A group of four to six members will sit in a row. For this exercise, the detective will be referred to as "he." The detective will either turn away or leave the room momentarily. The other members will decide who will be given a penny or a metal coin to hide in the hand.

Only one person will have a penny hidden in his or her hand. That person will make two fists, enclosing the penny in one fist so no one can tell in which hand the penny is held. The others will also close their hands as if they are holding the penny. After the penny is concealed in one hand, the detective is called back into the room. Any remaining members may act as the audience. They may assist by sending energy with upturned palms toward the detective or the person hiding the penny. They may also mentally project thoughts as clues to the detective.

The Detective

It's the detective's responsibility to select which hand holds the penny. He will relax his body by taking a long, deep breath and voiding his mind of all thoughts. At first, this may seem difficult, as many thoughts continue to pop into his head. The detective should not use logic. He will approach each member sitting in the row. He may look with open eyes or from time to time, close his eyes to sense within.

The detective should ask each person, "Do you have the penny?" He is to determine which vibrations are positive, therefore truthful, or which are negative, therefore deceitful. He will do this by feeling or sensing the aura of each hand. He may approach each member, place his hand over the member's hand, and feel or sense the aura energy.

Again, the detective should ask, "Do you have the penny?"

Each member will answer, "No, I don't have the penny." Obviously, one person is lying.

The detective may ask or do any of the following:

- Ask, "Do you have the penny in this hand?" The detective may move his hands over each member's hand while searching for a different sensation or feeling. The person who is lying may emit a cold or hot feeling, indicating a change of normal energy.
- Trace the energy of each hand until a slight pull is felt at a specific hand.
- Use the left or right hand or use both hands at one time.
- Sense if he is being drawn toward one person or hand.
- Sense any atmospheric change, such as a slight breeze or coolness in one member's hand.
- Move his hand slowly over each member, focusing on the energy of each aura.
- Again ask, "Do you have the penny?" Watch for a gray aura over the liar's head.
- With eyes closed, use the mind's eyes to observe if the aura is gray (a lie) or white (the truth).
- Move his hands above and around each person's body, feeling the aura for an irritating feeling. A lie or negative vibration may feel dull, sticky, irritating, nervous, jittery, or just an empty feeling, void of any positive energy.

- Close his eyes from time to time to allow images or symbols to form in his mind's eye, which will direct him toward the liar.
- Again ask, "Do you have the penny?" Listen for a guilty or higher pitch in the voice.
- Again ask, "Do you have the penny?" Watch the person's eyes, noting whether they reveal a guilty or negative feeling.
- Mentally request any spirit guides for help in determining who is lying.
- Notice or sense if he is being pushed away or drawn forward by the guides.
- Do not use logic.

Never waste energy by self-doubt, embarrassment, or feeling self-conscious. Each exercise should be fun. Don't feel you are competing against others. You are not being tested. You are gaining sensitivity and, in turn, a closer relationship with your own spiritual guides. Each person should take a turn until all have experienced how to detect a liar. After each exercise, the group should discuss how each had sensed the lie and the method used. Each person may have used a different technique to evaluate a liar. Learn from each other. Share information freely. Soon, each member will be able to detect a liar by several different methods. Repeat this exercise often until each has accomplished the technique of sensing by feeling with the hand. Repetition increases confidence and sensitivity.

Each time this exercise is repeated, different members should form a group. Some members will work better with one person as opposed to another, because they have like-energy. With practice, this exercise should strengthen your psychic awareness, and it will become easier to recognize your personal guides. Sensitivity of the hand is a forerunner to the next exercise, "How to Find a Lost Object."

Begin exercise.

Group Discussion Checklist
Did you feel any difference in each person's aura? Explain.
Did the liar's hand feel different? If so, how?
Which techniques worked best for you? Explain why.
Did you sense your personal guides assisting? If so, how?
What, if any, symbols or images came to mind?

Have you noticed a closer connection with your guardian angels?
Have you noticed a closer connection with your personal guides?
Discuss how detecting a liar can be useful in your daily life.

Which of the first seven exercises did the group find most interesting? Why?

Which exercise did the group find most valuable? Why?

Like-Minded Guides

Because you're growing spiritually, you will attract guides who are like-minded to your development. Like draws like. Keep your principles pure, and your guidance will be similar. As your awareness expands, new guides may join your personal guides. Each time you begin a new venture, a spirit guide with that specific talent may enter your energy field to assist you. Guides will come close to your energy field to inspire your decision as a thought or an inspiration. Each time your guides assist, your mind is strengthened by repetition, and your communication with the spirit world will improve.

Group Discussion Checklist

Are you aware of a spirit guide who has assisted you in a specific assignment?

Do you see or sense a spirit guide when working on a specific career?

What meditation or exercise has strengthened your awareness to your spirit guides?

Do you ever ask for help when drawing, sewing, painting, or repairing household articles?

Chapter 8
HOW TO FIND A LOST OBJECT

Have you ever lost your keys, wallet, or a piece of jewelry and couldn't remember where you lost it? Even though you don't recall where you placed the object, the subconscious mind has retained the information, including the sequence of how and where the object had been placed. Because it seemed inconsequential at the time, you dismissed it from your mind. And there it lies, hidden deep in the subconscious. You try to remember, but the harder you try, the more frustrated you become, blocking further recall. However, when the brain waves are slowed down and the right brain is alerted, then it's possible to reach into the subconscious and recall where you placed the object.

Let's examine your progress. The previous meditations and exercises were presented in a certain order best suited to strengthen specific psychic abilities. Meditation was introduced to create white-light protection and relax the physical body. You learned about brain waves and how to activate the intuitive right side of the brain. The meditations became more complex, and the third eye was awakened. Soon, you were able to see within the mind's eye. With each meditation, your visualization increased, and you became aware of symbols, images, and emotions. Visualization increased your ability to perform psychometry. The Black Box exercise prepared you to read vibrations by using your third eye. It also tested your ability to feel vibrations with your ethereal hands. You also experienced how the mind has the power to move the physical body. You became aware of your guides' gentle touch. Then you became the receiver and learned how to tune into the sender's vibrations as you were mentally nudged in a certain direction. This increased communication with your personal guides. You became aware of their presence and began to sense their gentle nudges. In the previous exercise, Sense a Liar, you learned how to recognize a negative energy (a lie) from positive energy (the truth).

Personal List

By now, you may have reviewed your personal list several times and found some fears or issues have been lessened or can be crossed off your list. You're not sure when or how those fears vanished, but they no longer exist. The answer may lie with the group discussions. Perhaps some fears had been released while listening to others discuss how they released their fears. By listening to another person's experience, you gain more confidence. If another member had communicated with his or her guides, so can you. Exchanging information helps to verify that we are all guided by loving, spiritual beings. There is a saying: "Energy flows where attention goes." So turn your attention toward your guides more often, and you will strengthen your contact with them.

Group Discussion Checklist

Have you eliminated a fear or doubt from your personal list?

What group discussion helped release a specific fear? Explain.

Have you added new questions to your personal list? If so, what new questions have you asked?

Have you gained a greater peace of mind in your daily life?

Have you noticed you have less anxiety or fear in your life?

The following exercise will present techniques to further strengthen an awareness of your guides. Perhaps you are wondering if you could someday assist the police in locating a specific person. Spiritual guidance would be necessary if you choose to assist in solving a crime. Each time you repeat this exercise, you are strengthening physical and metaphysical contact with your spirit guides. You are learning to notice their touch and gentle guidance.

Exercise. How to Find a Lost Object

A group of five or more people is needed to create enough energy to perform the next exercise. The group will sit in a circle to hold in the group's energy. The larger the group, the more energy created. Before beginning meditation, the group should mentally surround the circle with God light or recite a prayer of protection. You may use Meditation to Create God Light Protection or any prayer intuitively received.

An object, such as a spoon, a penny, or any metal object, is passed around to each member. Metal is preferred because it holds a stronger vibration than cloth or paper. Each person will take a turn holding the object. They may close their eyes, take a deep breath, slow down their brain waves, and then tune into the object's vibrations. Some may prefer to hold the object in the left hand or against the forehead. Some may visualize the object in the mind's eye. Take a moment or two to mentally tune into the object and then pass it to the next person until all have tuned into the same object.

For this exercise, we will refer to the *finder* as he. The finder will either turn his back or leave the room momentarily. The object is then placed somewhere within the circle, but it must not be visible. It may be placed under a shoe, on a chair, on the floor, held in the hand, sat upon, or hidden in a pocket. The finder is asked to return to the room. He will stand in the center of the circle, take a deep breath, and slowly exhale until he reaches his own level of awareness.

The finder may use any or all of these methods:

- Stand in the center of the circle until he mentally receives guidance toward the object.
- Close his eyes and sense if his body is being nudged.
- Allow his body to sway with the movement.
- Sense or notice if his body is leaning. Take several steps toward the direction the body is leaning and then pause. When the body again begins to lean, he should take another step, following his body as it leans toward the hidden object.
- Feel or sense if he is being guided toward a specific area of the circle or toward a certain person. He should move with this feeling, one step at a time. Wait until his body feels a pushing or pulling motion and then step toward the movement.

- Close his eyes from time to time to see symbols within the mind's eye. The symbols will direct him toward the object.
- Symbols may appear as a bright light or a shimmering arrow pointing toward the object.
- Mentally ask his guides to create an image or symbol. Use this symbol as a future reference.
- Allow his hand to intuitively rise and point toward the hidden object. Follow the hand's direction.
- If he feels he has made a mistake, it's okay to step into the center of the circle and start again.
- Some members will reach for the object without hesitation. Some will know exactly where the object is, even before they enter the circle. Their attention will immediately be drawn toward the person holding the object.

The group may:

- With palms turned up, send energy toward the finder.
- Assist by telepathically directing the finder.
- Send thoughts of pushing or drawing the finder in the direction of the object.
- Send an image of the person who is holding the object.
- Send a thought of directing energy to the person holding the object.

After the finder has located the object, it's now his turn to hide the object. Each person should take a turn until each has attempted to locate the object. After the exercise is completed, it's important to discuss the technique each found most helpful and whether a guide led him/her toward the object. Learn from each other. The more you share and give freely, the more you will receive. Next time you lose something, just stand in the center of a room, call upon your spiritual guidance, and wait to be guided.

Begin meditation. Begin exercise to find the object.

Group Discussion Checklist

Did you feel your body leaning? Did you follow the movement?

Did you feel you were guided in a certain direction?

Did you sense or feel your guides assisting you?

Did your spirit guides mentally convey a message?

What, if any, symbol was received, and how was it analyzed?

What technique did you find most useful?

Did you find yourself doubting your ability?

Has this exercise increased your awareness of spiritual assistance? How?

Did you remember to thank your guides and angels? If not, mentally do so now.

In the previous exercise, you knew what the object was and approximately where it was hidden. However, there may come a time when someone will ask you to find a lost object, something you have never seen before. Certainly, the memory of such an object is not in your subconscious. You're not even sure what it looks like. How then would you find such an object?

When a person misplaces an article, the subconscious mind remembers the last site of the article. All information that is retained in the person's memory is also accessible through the person's aura. Additionally, the vibratory energy of that memory is impressed in anything that person was wearing at the time of the loss. By using psychometry, the reader can tune into the person's aura or an article of clothing he or she was wearing when the article was lost and then find it.

The following story is a true psychic experience showing how psychometry was used to find a lost bracelet. The names have been changed to protect the privacy of those involved.

The Bracelet

Bonnie was curious about psychic phenomena and asked her friend, Sue, who is psychic, to use psychometry to find a gold bracelet she had lost. Bonnie remembered where she had last worn the bracelet, and thought it was lost outside her house.

"Yes, of course, I'll try," said Sue. "Let me hold your watch or glasses. I'll read from them."

Bonnie slipped off her watch and handed it to Sue. "I think I lost the bracelet outside my house. That was the last time I wore it."

Sue took a deep breath and lowered her brain waves. She wasn't sure she could do this because it was not a serious matter. Usually, she did better at psychometry if the matter was of a more serious nature, but she felt she should try. Sue had known Bonnie only a short time and knew very little about her personal life. Sue closed her eyes and fingered Bonnie's watch to pick up its vibrations. Pictures began to form in her mind's eye. "I see a colonial house. Do you live in a large, white colonial?"

"Yes," Bonnie answered.

This confirmation told Sue she was on the right track. It strengthened the communication and encouraged Sue to continue. "I'm in a bedroom at the back of this house. There's a closet to the right of me as I enter the room."

Bonnie interrupted. "My bedroom is at the back of the house, and my closet is to the right of the doorway."

"All right. Now I'm looking at the top shelf of a closet. I see a box or square container. Inside this container is another container … cloth. It has a pocket."

Bonnie again interrupted. "I have a suitcase on the top shelf of my closet. Could this be what you're seeing?"

"I don't know," Sue answered. "I can only tell you what I see. This other container has a pocket like a purse or something." Sue only saw fragments of a pocket against a black background. She sensed this pocket belonged to a softer, smaller container stored within a larger, harder container.

"I don't keep my purses on the top shelf of the closet," Bonnie interrupted.

"Okay. Now I'm seeing a white sweater. Yarn … a white yarn sweater," Sue said as she sensed white yarn against the black background.

"I don't keep my sweaters on the top shelf of the closet, either," Bonnie insisted, sure this was wrong. She had never remembered putting a sweater on that shelf.

"All right. But try not to give me negative answers. They tend to turn me off. Let's just see where this goes." Sue took another deep breath and searched the darkness of her mind's eye. "I sense it's a white sweater in this pocket," she said. It seemed illogical that a sweater could fit in a pocket, but she shrugged her shoulders and continued, "I see a gold bracelet caught in this white sweater, something about the yarn of the white sweater. I can't be sure what this means, but I feel this is where your gold bracelet is. I'm sorry. That's all I see."

"I'll look in my closet, but I don't have purses or sweaters on that shelf," Bonnie insisted. She left disappointed, sure Sue had been mistaken about everything she had seen. There wasn't much hope in her voice as she said good-bye.

Later that day, Bonnie phoned Sue from home. "I found my bracelet," she chattered excitedly. "It was on the top shelf of the closet just like you said. It was in a suitcase. Inside that suitcase was my purse. So I looked in the side pocket of the purse, and there it was. You know what's so strange? The bracelet was caught on a piece of white yarn."

"That must be the white sweater I saw. The yarn, I mean," Sue said.

"Yes," answered Bonnie. "My bracelet must have snagged that strand of yarn off my sweater."

Explanation

Sue performed psychometry using Bonnie's watch to tune into the vibrations that surrounded Bonnie at the time she lost her bracelet. Often, our minds subconsciously see things we do not consciously see. This was the case when the gold bracelet was lost. Bonnie subconsciously knew where she had last seen her bracelet. Her subconscious registered the bracelet in the pocket of her purse. She had absentmindedly put her purse in the suitcase. This was not something she normally would do. She also may have seen the bracelet caught on her sweater but dismissed the incident because it seemed inconsequential at the time.

This sequence of events registered in Bonnie's aura, and the vibrations clung to the articles of clothing she was wearing at the time. Therefore, Bonnie's watch contained the vibrations that paralleled what was on her mind at the time (i.e., the loss of her gold bracelet). This reading was not magic, simply the reading of impressions in the energy field surrounding Bonnie's watch … and not very strange at all.

Group Discussion Checklist

Have you lost an article only to remember where it is when you are relaxed or nearly asleep?

Do you get answers to problems when nearly asleep or at rest?

Have you dreamed of where you had placed a lost article?

Chapter 9
VISUALIZING A PAST LIFE

The conscious and subconscious minds hold memories of our present life experiences. However, deep within our super-subconscious mind are memories of past-life experiences, often referred to as cell memories. Each cell in our body has a consciousness that retains memories of our present and past lives. Although we are not consciously aware, the accumulation of those experiences has influenced us, making each of us a unique person. That is why people, even twins who are born under the same zodiac sign, may be quite different.

But why should we be interested in our past lives? What can we learn by uncovering memories of the past? And how will these help our present lives?

When visualizing a past life, we will use our mind's eye to observe, as if we were an outsider looking in. We will see what we had done and what we had failed to do in the past. With each past-life regression, we will understand how those experiences have shaped our present belief systems. We will recognize what motivates our habits, fears, and even our points of view. As we review each past-life incarnation, we may find we lived with different personalities, ideologies, and mannerisms. We may have acted under common or uncommon beliefs. We may have walked many different paths and lived in various locations of the world. Would it surprise you to know some of us may have existed on known or unknown planets within or outside of this galaxy?

Our soul is continually climbing the spiritual ladder toward oneness with God. As we review our past lives, we will begin to understand the origin of any defects we may be dealing with in this present life. Each past-life regression will reveal a part of how we came to be as we are.

What We Learn from a Past Life

While observing a past life, we may discover we had lived as a master, ruled as a judge, or led a country to battle. We may have been gifted, talented, poor, or abused. Some cell memories may be positive, and some negative. Certain cell memories may be powerful enough to influence us to fail or drive us to succeed in this present life.

As an example, we may come upon a past life similar to our current life situation. It may be a financial problem, a love issue, or a flaw in our personality that prevents us from achieving our full potential. We realize our present problem includes the same fears that we had experienced in a past life. A past-life memory can influence the point of view that guides our present life decisions. Memories of failure can remain a part of our personalities. A memory is a thought pattern. Thoughts make decisions. Through regression, each person will have a chance to review several past lives. Now armed with the knowledge of what mistakes we had made, we can change errors in our present life. It is a choice.

It isn't a coincidence you are in this class at this time, reviewing your past lives. With this new information, you will be better able to confront daily problems with clarity, understanding, and compassion. You will learn to face and then change your thinking process, thereby changing the outcome of your present life situation. When we heal our past errors, we heal our future lives.

There are many reasons why a person may reincarnate to experience the same situation over and over again:

- A person may reincarnate in hopes of overcoming a specific fear, failure, or personality flaw.
- A person may be in a rut. His or her memories are stuck in a replay of the past.
- A person may revisit a failure to amend the harm he/she had done to another.
- A person may relive the same negative situation because he/she is comfortable with its familiarity.
- A person may be unable to release a past-life memory, so he/she surrenders to the same situation again.

Because a person is living a difficult life doesn't mean he/she is being punished by God. A soul may choose to reincarnate into a difficult life situation as an opportunity to learn forgiveness and compassion. Often, when life has brought people to their knees, they find they must reach out to others for compassion. This is a beautiful lesson. When people experience what it is to be needy, they are quicker to respond to others with more tolerance. Compassion toward others is a Godlike quality that brings people closer to the God consciousness.

Group Discussion Checklist

Examine each issue so each person may contribute an interesting confirmation of past lives.

Do you believe you have lived before? If so, why?

As a child, did you enjoy studying the history of a certain country or culture?

Do you remember certain grade school history classes easily? Why?

Did it seem natural to learn about a specific country or culture?

What grade school subject were you drawn to? Why?

Do you believe you had a past life in a specific country or culture? If so, explain.

Do you have a natural talent or one inherited through family genes?

What likes or dislikes do you suspect were caused by a past life?

Do you have an unresolved fear?

Is it possible a present fear was caused by a past life? If so, explain.

Do you know or suspect you are currently living a specific situation as a way to learn?

Have you had a fleeting memory or a déjà vu moment of a similar situation?

Are you ready to forgive yourself for any past-life errors?

Red Light Reveals Past-Life Memories

Each person will have a turn sitting in front of the room with a red light shining upon his or her face. For this exercise, one person will be known as the *sitter*. The remaining members will be known as the *viewers*. A red light is used to amplify the viewing of a past life. An ordinary red light-bulb may be purchased at a local store. A small lamp containing the red light-bulb is placed on a chair. A cloth may be draped across the back of a chair, or a piece of cardboard is placed in front of the lamp to shield the light from the viewers. The lamp is placed so the light will shine upward upon the sitter's face.

The spectrum of red light blending with the sitter's aura vibrations will create reflections and shadows flashing in and out across the sitter's face. The group's energy will increase the viewer's ability to see or sense an illusion of facial features upon the sitter's face. The larger the group, the more energy created. It's not known why the human eye reacts psychically to the waves of the red spectrum or how the red rays and aura vibrations create a facial illusion. However, from experience, the red light is successful in creating an illusion of facial impressions.

The viewers may sense or see dark and light shadows moving swiftly across the sitter's face. And within those shadows, they may see or sense an impression of facial features belonging to a past life. The viewers will sense the facial imprint rather than actually see it. The right side of the brain, the intuitive brain, comes into play and will sense and then intuitively translate the shadows as a past-life memory.

At first, the novice might only observe the dark and light shadows as a slight warp across the sitter's face. However, as the energy in the room increases, the novice will begin to see or sense the transformations more easily. Most viewers will observe facial changes with eyes open. However, the novice should close his or her eyes from time to time and use the third eye to see or sense intuitively.

The Sitter

For this exercise, the sitter will be known as *she*. The sitter is seated in the front of the room with a red light shining upon her face. She will mentally say a prayer, asking her angels and guides for "protection, guidance, and directions." She may keep her eyes open or close the eyes from time to time. The head should be held upright, and the back straight. She should not slouch or cross the legs. Crossing the ankles is permitted as this does not twist the spine and does not stop the natural flow of energy through the body.

The sitter will close her eyes and lower brain waves by taking several slow, deep breaths. With each exhale, she will sense her body relaxing. She will mentally draw upon the energy the group is sending with upturned hands. She will use her mind and her thoughts to draw a past life forward. The vibrations emanating from her cell memories, when combined with the spectrum of red light, can be seen by the human eye or in the mind's eye. A sitter with a strong aura energy will produce clearer vibrations, making it easier for a novice to see or sense the changing facial features. The list of possible scenarios is listed below. The list is intentionally long and will allow the sitter to understand the different scenes, situations, or past lives that he or she may observe while in meditation.

- There may come a time when an experienced sitter will see or sense, within her mind's eye, the same past-life memory that the viewers are observing. The viewer's comments will confirm the identity of that specific past life. However, most of the time, it's the viewers who describe the changes as they flash across the sitter's face.

- A past life may appear cloaked in a different body, living a different lifestyle or working out a specific life problem. The viewers may see or sense bits and pieces of the sitter's past life or only a brief portion of an unpleasant past life. It is those negative memories the sitter should be eager to recall. Each time a negative past life is brought forward, a recognition of that existence could release fragments of fear or a portion of the trauma that had occurred during that lifetime. Extremely difficult past-life experiences should be reviewed several times in order to release a specific fear or phobia.

- While viewing a past life, both the sitter and the viewers should offer compassion and forgiveness for whatever appears. It doesn't matter who the sitter was in a past life or what she had endured. It is done! She should release it! The very act of releasing negative memories will bring honor to the self; and honoring the self is honoring the soul's purpose.

- The sitter should mentally tell her mind she is using the red light's vibrations to review a past-life memory. The mind must know what it is doing.

The following list is just a few suggestions of what can or may be asked. Discuss the list thoroughly before sitting in front of the red light.

- The sitter may mentally say, "I am going back ... back ... back in time to a past life." Allow time to drift backward. Sense or feel the body drifting back. The sitter may mentally request angels and guides to act as escorts to a past life.
- Mentally or verbally say, "I wish to bring forward a past-life memory that will benefit my present life. Thank you, God, for this energy and information."
- Mentally or verbally say, "I wish to bring forward a past-life memory that has caused fear of (name a person, fear, or phobia). Thank you, God, for this energy and information."
- The sitter may mentally or verbally say, "I wish to bring forward a past-life memory to expand my (name the talent). I wish to increase and retain the knowledge of (talent). Thank you, God, for this energy and information."
- A sitter may feel or sense a facial feature. She may say, "I feel oriental." Or, "I feel I am tall, happy, or sad." She should speak her feelings in a low voice. If she speaks with excitement, this may cause her brain waves to rise, and she will lose the ability to see within the mind's eye.
- The sitter may express what she is observing within her mind's eye a different body, race, culture, or ethnic awareness.
- The sitter may sense the gender. Is she male or female?
- The sitter may have the ability to sense her own past life. She may see, with closed eyes, images within her mind's eye. She may see and feel physical changes. Her face may feel quite different from her own. Her mouth may feel larger or smaller. Her eyes may feel squinted, larger, or smaller. Or she may sense it is difficult to see, as if she had been blind in a previous life. Sometimes the sitter will feel her eyes are open, even though the physical eyes are closed.
- The shadows and reflections will move rapidly across the face. The emotions and feelings will last only seconds. The sitter should comment on the changes as she feels or senses them crossing her face.
- Not all will see or sense the same changes as the shadows move rapidly across the sitter's face. Those who are less intuitive may only see or sense slight changes. The viewers should comment on the changes as the shadows appear and disappear quickly.

Because the same lines or shadows are not seen by all, this gives proof the viewing is not just a physical anomaly.

- The sitter should mentally inform her guides and angels that she wishes to project only one past-life memory at a time. However, sometimes the sitter will project several past lives that spontaneously flash in and out quickly, without the sitter's recognition.

- Rapid eye movement (REM) is a good indication the sitter is seeing within the mind's eye.

- If the sitter feels the group is asking too many questions, she should hold her hand up, motioning for the questions to stop.

- A sitter may appear to have eyes open, even though the eyes are actually closed. The sitter should notice at whom her eyes seem to stare. This may be an intuitive recognition of a past life.

- Sometimes the sitter may feel a specific past life is uncomfortable or not important. She should mentally tell her guides or angels she does not wish to continue. She should then take a deep breath and breathe herself back to the present time. Or she may inform the group she wishes to release this past life and return to the present.

- The sitter should be prepared for any traumatic event that could present itself. She must mentally remind herself she is only viewing a past-life memory. She must be able to quickly release the traumatic memory with love and understanding to the God light.

- When viewing a past tragedy, the sitter must remind herself she is no longer that same person. She should honor herself with forgiveness for what she had caused or had endured in the past. She may mental or verbally respond, "It is done! I release all (name of fears) to the God light."

When the sitter is ready to return to the present time, she may do any of the following:

- Take a deep breath and mentally command herself to come forward to the present time.
- Mentally wrap herself in the God light or white light, take a deep breath, and open her eyes.

- The sitter may use any taught method or one she receives intuitively.
- If a death or traumatic scene presents itself, the sitter should rise above the drama. She should observe the tragedy without emotion so she can truly appreciate what had happened in the past. She should notify the group of the traumatic situation and then mentally repeat to herself, "I am rising above. Rising up ... up. I am above the scene. I am only observing. I am only observing."
- If the group recognizes the sitter is overwhelmed by the trauma or has been unable to rise above the scene, one person should assist by saying, "You are rising above the scene. You are only observing. You are only observing. Rising up. Rising up. You feel no emotion to that experience. You are coming back. On the count of three, you will return to the present time. One, coming back. Two, coming back. Three. Open your eyes."

The sitter should release any negative memories before returning to the present. She can clear away any unwanted memories by doing the following:

- The sitter may move her hands across her body to lift any unwanted memories from her aura. The movement will appear as if taking off a sweater.
- Mentally ask all negative past-life memories be released before coming back to the present; it is not necessary to hang on to any more old baggage.
- The sitter may use any taught method or one intuitively received. Each person may use a different method.

The Viewer

The viewers will lower their brain waves, mentally draw white light energy into the top of their heads through their bodies, and direct it out their hands as a continuous stream of energy toward the sitter. This energy will help the sitter and the viewers to see or sense a past life. Some viewers may prefer to sit on the floor rather than on a chair. When the eyes are cast upward, as if looking at the top of a mountain, the brain waves tend to slow down more easily, allowing extrasensory perception (ESP) to take place.

- The viewer's questions should be kept at a minimum. They should ask only one question at a time.
- Because the sitter has lowered her brain waves, she may have difficulty speaking. So, don't press for an answer.
- Viewers should not interrupt the sitter. They should be patient, giving the sitter plenty of time to feel the emotion of the scene.
- Viewers should softly discuss the reflective lines, shadows, or features as they flash rapidly across the sitter's face.
- Viewers may sense a traumatic scene unfolding. They should describe the trauma or scene. They should allow time for the sitter to release the scene to the God light.
- Viewers should mentally request any angels or personal guides to assist in releasing a negative memory from the sitter.
- Viewers may see a white or translucent ball of energy floating over the sitter's head. A ball of energy or sphere of light may be an angel, a guide, a visiting spirit, or a cell memory of a past life. The viewers should explain the message they are intuitively receiving from the ball of light.
- Viewers should not startle the sitter by coughing or laughing loudly.
- If a comical facial expression or peculiar life experience appears, the viewers must maintain self-control. There should be no loud reaction to comical expressions. Chuckling softly is permitted while expressing your opinion. Not all lives have been serious or dramatic.

Now that you understand how vibrations can be seen, it's time to observe those vibrations through the red light. The group will go down in meditation. Any meditation may be used. "Body Relaxation Meditation" or "Meditation to Increase Visualization" are suggested. Or the group may select a meditation they all agree would be most effective.

Past-life readings may be repeated several times, as long as the group agrees they are interesting and constructive and offer valuable guidance for their present lives. Each time this exercise is repeated, the members may select a different meditation. Meditation increases awareness, alertness, intelligence, creativity, and stability and strengthens psychic ability.

Exercise 1. Red Light Viewing

The sitter is seated in the front of the room with a red light upon her face. Each person should mentally call upon his or her guides and angels for protection, guidance, and directions. The room should be semi-dark. The lamp should be lit before class begins. This will allow the spectrum of red light to increase the energy within the room.

Begin meditation. Begin Red Light Viewing.

Group Discussion Checklist

Did you see or sense shadows or lines creating facial features?

What feature was most clear?

Did you see or sense a face with a different ethnicity? If so, explain.

Did you close your eyes and look within?

Did you sense or feel an emotion of a past life?

What impressed you the most?

After each exercise, remember to check your personal list.

Before viewing a past life for a second time, please read the following to become familiar with other aspects of past-life viewing.

How a Past Life Could Affect a Present Life

As a sitter revisits several past lives, she may encounter good or bad experiences. If a past experience had been traumatic, that trauma could remain hidden within the super-subconscious mind as a cell memory. She may not consciously recall the trauma or understand that it can cause stress upon her physical body, emotions, and nervous system or how it could alter her present point of view.

A traumatic past-life experience could cause an irrational fear, such as feeling uneasy with certain types of people, fashions, or customs, or a sensitivity to certain foods. She may have a dislike or fear of a certain person seemingly without cause or valid justification.

For example, consider a person who had been hanged or guillotined in a past life. That person may feel uncomfortable in a turtleneck sweater, a tie, or a scarf tied about the neck. Or a person who had drowned in a past life might feel uncomfortable in a boat or around water activities. If that person had experienced the same tragic drowning in many lifetimes, those memories may remain strongly bonded within the cells. The fear of water-related events will remain until the fear has been released. Each past life reviewed will allow the sitter an opportunity to face a fear and release it to the God light.

On the other hand, a pleasant past-life memory could pique an interest in learning more about a specific talent or occupation. It could even affect the way a person acts, talks, or dresses. In grade school, a child may have shown an interest in the history of a specific country because he/she had once lived in such a place. That cell memory may remain in the super-subconscious. A person may be drawn to a certain lifestyle because he/she still feels comfortable with that pleasant lifetime. Perhaps a person had lived many past lives performing a specific talent. That talent may manifest itself in this present life. This could be one explanation as to why a child protégé may excel at a talent even though that child had little or no training.

Group Discussion Checklist
Does a specific historical event interest you?
Do you feel you had lived during a historical event?
Have you experienced déjà vu? If so, explain.
What grade school subject was most memorable?
What country or nationality seems most interesting or appealing?
Do you have a gifted talent not learned?
Have you had a dream regarding the talent you were born with?
Do you feel uncomfortable with a specific person, certain styles of clothing, or furniture? Explain.
Does a relative, friend, or acquaintance seem familiar? Explain.

Past-life memories are recalled in different ways:

- A past-life memory can be experienced in a dream state. Those dreams usually appear in color, are more vivid, and are easily recalled.
- Past-life memories may also appear as déjà vu; they may come as

a glimpse of "I've been there before." Or, for just a split second, an image from the past may flash before your eyes, and there is a remembrance of some sort.

- A glimpse of a past-life event may be seen or sensed while deep in meditation, with or without invitation or summoning on your part.
- A past-life memory can be sensed or seen in the mind's eye. Always ask your guides and angels to assist when reviewing a past life while in meditation.
- A past life can also be reviewed while laying down in meditation. The prone position allows the body to relax more completely, thus allowing the mind to recall a past life with deeper clarity.
- A past life can be viewed while seated in front of a mirror, with a red light shining upon his or her face. The red spectrum of light will cast dark and light shadows. The person will intuitively interpret the facial features of past lives as they move quickly across the face.

Why a Soul Reincarnates

During some incarnations, we may have lost sight of our spiritual goal. We may have distanced ourselves from the knowledge that we are divine beings and were once connected to the original source, the God consciousness. Life is a continuum, an everlasting growth of the soul. Each incarnation presents us with an opportunity to regain that spiritual knowledge.

There are other reasons why a soul reincarnates. Some souls enjoy the challenge of living. Some return to fulfill a contract, strengthen a weakness, or correct a previous injustice. Souls often return in groups, joining with family or friends whom they had known during many, many lifetimes. They may still feel the bond and may still have contracts to work out or relationships to complete.

Because we have lived many lives, we may not have always been the best we could be. There may have been times when we had done harm to others or had acted without compassion for our fellow human beings. Therefore, some may choose to or be required to reincarnate to comprehend the injustices they had committed against another. It's reasonable to assume we have experienced many different circumstances.

This present life will add another new experience. How we handle this present life experience will affect our future incarnations. The soul understands the cosmic law of cause and effect. The soul wants to clean the slate for its next incarnation.

A question often asked by my students is, "What happens to those who commit suicide? How does God judge them?"

It is my belief that God doesn't punish a person for errors of judgment. That person—his or her higher self—will find a way to correct his or her own errors of judgment. Through my personal communication with a person who committed suicide, I have come to the conclusion that a person who commits suicide often desires to reincarnate quickly. This may be because after the soul entered the God light, it realized suicide had not solved the problem. Suicide only had only postponed the problem. A soul may wish to reincarnate quickly to correct the error.

Group Discussion Checklist

Do you feel you are being challenged to resolve a specific issue with a friend or family member?

How has a friend, family member, or teenager challenged your patience?

Do you believe you have had a past life with a relative or friend?

Do you believe a soul may reincarnate for the joy of experiencing life?

Do you believe a soul may want to reincarnate to continue along the path of learning?

Give other explanations for reincarnation.

Spirit Visitation

Not all souls exist in the dimension closest to the earthly world. Some may have risen to a finer, more celestial dimension, one closer to the God consciousness. After passing into the God light, most souls exist in an extremely light, heavenly dimension. They adjust to the weightlessness and the ability to move instantly from one place to another on the wings of a thought. While the soul resides in its appropriate dimension, it begins to revert to its youthful age of approximately thirty. However, when visiting loved ones in the physical world, the soul, now known as a spirit, may not always appear in its youthful state. If a spirit visits the earth plane, it may show itself so it is easily recognized. It may express itself with its previous personality. The spirit's visit will be brief, usually with a message of love.

A spirit may visit its loved ones or observe family gatherings. It doesn't usually interact with the family or remain for long periods, because any interaction with the physical world would now be very different. A spirit encounters the earthly dimension as dense or heavy much like a human would if pulled down by extreme gravity. Therefore, any extended interaction with the physical world requires additional energy. An earthly visit can drain the spirit's energy, tiring it quickly. That's why most spirits seem impatient and want to be heard quickly. They wish to return to the serenity of their own dimension. A spirit may communicate briefly if the receiver is sensitive enough to receive its message. Spirit communication usually occurs as the living lower their brain waves ready to sleep or are in a relaxed state of mind.

Group Discussion Checklist

Have you experienced a loved one's visitation?

Have you felt the cold chill of a spirit's presence?

Have you felt your hair touched or lifted by a spirit?

Have you felt a spirit's presence as cobwebs on your face?

Has a spirit tried to get your attention by touching you, as if a feather was brushing your face?

Have you experienced a spirit sitting on the edge of your bed?

How has a spirit made its presence known to you?

Light Workers

Some old souls reincarnate for the purpose of helping the living become aware of the God consciousness. They are known as light workers. They may have been light workers in many past lives and have returned to earth to assist others. When reviewing your past lives, you may learn that a part of your present life assignment may be that of a light worker. With that, you have the honor of teaching others, thus taking part in raising the earth's vibrations to a finer, more harmonious planet.

Light workers make a mental effort to create billions of positive vibrations each time they meditate or speak with honorable intentions. They project their positive thoughts into the universe. Those billions of positive thoughts have the power to change the earth's vibration to a finer, lighter degree. This accumulation of positive energy will eventually bring about the thinning of the veil between the lower dimension (earth) and the higher dimension (heaven). This thinning of the veil will make it easier for physical bodies to contact spirit bodies. Light workers are assisting in the unification of the dimensions. The merger of the dimension will increase a person's ability to contact the spirit world and the celestial dimensions more easily.

Group Discussion Checklist

Do you believe you are a light worker?

Do you mentally send peace, love, harmony, and God's light toward others and into the earth?

What positive results can occur with the thinning of the veil between the earth and heaven?

Are you assisting in the unification of the earth's vibrations by sending out positive thoughts, sincere prayers, and compassion? Or do you do this through meditation? If so, share your knowledge of how others can assist in the unification of the earth's vibrations.

Transfiguration

A sitter with a strong energy field (aura) may transfigure a past-life memory. The transformation may appear as a transparent face superimposed like a veil over the sitter's face, or it may appear as a faint image standing beside or in front of the sitter. The sitter's aura and the spectrum of red light combined with the group's energy allows the cell memory to manifest itself. The sitter's energy is not siphoned or consumed by the spirit-like image. The aura is a vibratory energy the sitter has already discarded. The cell memory merely absorbs itself into the aura energy to make its presence visible. A transfiguration may be a spirit but is usually only a memory.

Sensing or Seeing Energy Thought Patterns

Each human thought produces an array of colorful aura vibrations, depending upon the intensity of the thought. Aura colors change daily. When a word is spoken, the mind reacts to the emotion of that word, producing colorful aura vibrations around the physical body. Thoughts are unspoken words that also emit aura vibrations. All words, thoughts, intentions, sounds, and actions contain energy that alters the color, hue, and intensity of the aura. Most aura colors are too subtle to be seen by the human eye. However, those colors do exist and can be visualized or sensed by the third eye.

Exercise 2. Red Light Reveals Past-Life Memories

Now that you understand more about what can occur in a past-life reading, the Red Light exercise should be repeated until each person feels comfortable with the process. Each sitting will bring a clearer recognition of your past lives. If your higher self (your soul) has a sincere desire to release a specific past-life memory, that desire will increase the energy, and the memory will present itself. This appears to work easily when the desire is of a spiritual nature, such as bringing a past life forward with the intention of learning your soul's purpose.

The sitter is seated in the front of the room with a red light shining upon his or her face. Each person should use a form of white-light protection or mentally call upon guides and angels for protection, guidance, and directions.

Begin preselected meditation. Begin this exercise, Red Light Reveals Past-Life Memories.

Group Discussion Checklist

While in the presence of the red light, what, if any, facial changes did you sense or feel?

Did you recognize whether you were a male or female?

Did you know in what country you had once lived?

Did you know what era you had once lived?

Did your interest in a specific historical event present itself as a past life?

Did you sense many past-life memories flashing in and out?

Did a viewer observe a transfiguration? If so, describe the image.

Did sitting on the floor improve your viewing?

Check Your Personal List

It's time to review your personal list. After having recalled several past lives, you may be surprised to find a number of fears or misconceptions can be crossed off your list. Your list may indicate a particular negative influence is no longer present or a phobia or fear has been lessened. Be sure to record how you came to release a specific fear or resentment.

Sometimes the fear will just disappear without any knowledge or effort on your part. The more details you record, the more you'll become aware of intimate details that you have stored in your super-subconscious.

Group Discussion Checklist
  Did you release any fears or phobias?
  Did you resolve any unanswered question that puzzled you?
  Do you now feel more at peace with a certain situation or person?
  Did you cross off any misconceptions from your personal list?

Chapter 10
REGRESSION INTO A PAST LIFE

It is my belief that each incarnation is designed to encounter certain lessons for the soul's spiritual development. Each lifetime is important, this life in particular, because your present thoughts and intentions will affect your next incarnation. By reviewing your past lives, you will have the opportunity to face your past errors and release the negative aspects of those experiences.

Regression into a past life requires quieting the mind and body to an alpha level of awareness. This is a deeper level than viewing a past life in the red light. When your mind and body are very relaxed, a past life can be envisioned or sensed in the mind's eye. You may recall a recent past life, or one that occurred hundreds or thousands of years ago. It doesn't matter how far away, or how long ago, the past life occurred. Time and space are irrelevant. The memory of many past lives is already present in your cells and in your super-subconscious mind.

When reviewing a past life, you may observe your own past life or one belonging to a parent, aunt, uncle, grandparent, or even great-grandparent. Because you have inherited some genes from your ancestors, you have also inherited some of their cell memories. Therefore, you may recall past lives that may or may not have been your own personal experiences but ones that belonged to relatives. Even though you may not have been involved in those past experiences, those cell memories may be strong enough to have influenced your personality or point of view.

Group Discussion Checklist

Do you have character traits similar to a parent, grandparent, or great-grandparent?

Do you look like any ancestor? Who?

Have you inherited any ancestral talents? What?

Are your likes and dislikes similar to any ancestor? If so, explain.

Explain how looking like a relative is different than acting like a relative.

Divisions in Universal Energy

In the beginning, the Earth's changes were in harmony with the universe. All planets were constantly changing. Even the upheaval of the Earth's crust was in harmony with the universal plan. However, humankind, not necessarily of the planet Earth, but all humankind in physical body, spirit, and other dimensions, began to act upon its own ego.

On Earth, man's self-centered thoughts began to divide the harmony of his own personal energy. His egotistical thoughts created human divisions, such as good and evil, rich and poor, smart and dumb, illness and wellness, etc. These egotistical vibrations soared into the astral plane, altering the harmony of the planet Earth and the universe.

A division is also known as a dimension. Dimensions have been and still are created by billions of different thoughts, intentions, and actions taken by those who are in harmony or disharmony with the universal law. Planets and people change, but the universal law of cause and effect does not change. Universal law is constant. Every action has a reaction. Every cause has an effect.

Group Discussion Checklist

How does a positive thought cause a positive effect?

How does a negative thought cause a negative effect?

Explain how a person's actions can create cause and effect.

Dimensions

While in a past-life regression, you may see in your mind's eye an unexplainable scene. Strange images may fade in and out of your mind's eye rapidly. The scene may pass by so quickly that you won't have time to realize you had just observed another dimension.

A dimension may appear as symbols, vibrations, mathematical calculations, hieroglyphics, unknown images, or vibrating energy. You may be observing another dimension, one capable of supporting life but not as humankind understands life to be. Even if you don't understand the meaning, don't dismiss it as illogical and, therefore, not real. After viewing such a dimension in the mind's eye, record the details of the scene, even though you didn't understand it. Perhaps in the future, that same dimension may present itself again with deeper clarity. Record the second experience. If you sincerely show an interest in learning more, the spirit world may communicate an explanation of those dimensions. The confirmation may come on the third or fourth regression. Or it may be verified in a vision, an intuition, or a dream.

Group Discussion Checklist

What unusual scene, symbol, or image have you seen within your mind's eye?

What symbols appeared clearly? Did you understand the symbol?

Do you believe you have once existed in another dimension?

Where the Soul Resides after Physical Death

Have you ever wondered what happens to people after physical death? Where do they go, and what do they do? Through years of collective experiences, I have put together my understanding of what happens after physical death of a body.

Upon physical death, the silver cord disconnects, releasing the soul and ethereal bodies from the physical body. The soul and ethereal bodies rise up and enter another dimension. The transition into the God light may occur within seconds, days, or longer.

Usually, a spirit enters a dimension according to its spiritual light or darkness of misdeeds. A spirit who is spiritually aware of the God consciousness will see the serenity and beauty of the dimension it has entered. God consciousness does not require a spirit to be of any specific faith, creed, or religion. A consciousness is an awareness, therefore, a state of being.

However, on one occasion, after attempting to communicate with a recently deceased man, I was told by the spirit world that because he had suffered a long illness before death, he needed time to regenerate. Perhaps he needed time to lose the memory of his long illness. In time, he will awake and will experience the wholeness of being a spirit. In human terms, the time may be weeks or months until the spirit awakens free of earthly thoughts and is directed by angels or the God light to its earned dimension.

Spirits may reside in different dimensions, yet most have the ability to communicate with other spirits outside their own dimensions.

For example, while on Earth, people of different faiths or ideologies are able to communicate with each other. They may not agree with each other. They may be adamant they are right in their belief systems. Therefore, they exist as specific dogmas have taught them to believe. Their beliefs are their own earthly dimensions. They see what they have been taught to see. They live as they believe they should live. They find it difficult to communicate with or understand another person's point of view.

However, people who are open-minded to all knowledge have a greater advantage because they examine differences without prejudice. They examine and then accept or reject portions of different belief systems. Because they are not closed-minded, they are open to new information that will benefit their present lives. The new knowledge may even change their ways of thinking or acting. Thereafter, the dimension they exist in after physical death will not be confined to only one fixed point of view.

While the spirit exists in its proper dimension, it may be schooled or involved in activities. It will have the opportunity to connect with spiritual assistance and to reflect upon its thoughts of guilt or fear. Spiritual assistance will help it realize its full worth. Eventually, after existing for a long time in the in-between existence, the spirit is advised which life experiences it will encounter in its next incarnation. It's not known whether the spirit makes the choice, or if it is chosen by God's spiritual council. The next incarnation may include issues necessary for spiritual growth.

There are always exceptions to the rule. After physical death, some spirits retain thoughts so powerful that those thoughts prevent them from entering the God light. They are known as *earthbound spirits*. A spirit's memory may be so firmly locked in its recent tragic passing that fear has prevented it from seeing the God light. Or some spirits are held earthbound by guilt or are not at peace with their conscience regarding previous life principles.

Some earthbound spirits are not willing to enter the unknown or leave their earthly treasures. These spirits often haunt houses or people because they simply don't know what else to do. Usually, earthbound spirits haunts to attract attention or want to be noticed for their own personal reasons. Most of the time, spirits are asking for prayers or requesting guidance to the God light.

Through my own experience of communicating with spirits, I have come across a spirit tumbling in darkness, unaware of where to go after physical death. He did not know what to do because, when he was alive, his church told him that he would sleep until God called him. Therefore, when this man passed over, he was caught in a man-made thought pattern that did not allow him to expect to see the God light. This teaching made it difficult for him to experience all that God has to offer. Fortunately, through prayer and mental communication, I was able to coax this man to the God light. Some spirits are unable to see the God light because they have been told or believe they are not worthy of God's love. This, of course, is not true. God's love and compassion is beyond human comprehension.

Group Discussion Checklist

How does a guilty thought create a thought pattern, a dimension?

How does a positive thought create a thought pattern, a dimension?

What is your definition of a dimension? Explain. Even this definition will change as your knowledge increases.

How does a fear or disbelief prevent a spirit from entering the God light?

Share what you have you learned or experienced regarding other dimensions.

Spiritual Dimensions

While on earth, most humans, with the exceptions of a very few, cannot see or sense where angels, archangels, and the ascended masters reside, because those masters exist in extremely fine dimensions close to the God consciousness. As humans, we know little of the celestial dimensions closest to God. We can only speculate. We live with the expectation that we may, one day, ascend to a finer dimension and communicate with the spiritual masters who are in service to God.

The peaceful dimension where angels dwell is a human interpretation of heaven. However, a person cannot begin to understand the true beauty, the peace, the vibrant colors, the harmony, the absolute compassion, and the unconditional love that exist in the dimension closest to the God consciousness. The power of absolute love and compassion would overwhelm the human mind. Heaven is more than words can express.

When viewing a past life, you may mentally request to observe a spiritual dimension in which you had once existed. The request must be asked with sincerity. The brain waves must be slowed down deep enough to recall such an ethereally fine dimension. Celestial cell memories are rare and difficult to recall. A view or sensing of a divine dimension will be very subtle, very brief, and very rare. If you are lucky, you may, for just a split second, recall the unconditional love and compassion of a heavenly dimension. This will be a truly life-changing experience. Be sure to thank your angels, guides, and God for so special a viewing.

The Dimension of My Heaven

One of the many dimensions a spirit may enter after physical death is the beautiful "Dimension of Unconditional Love." Through my communication with a young woman in the spirit world, she referred to this dimension as "my heaven." She described it as a dimension of beauty and absolute harmony. She mentally conveyed to me, through automatic writing, that in this dimension, there are no words. The spirits convey the messages by projecting emotions, which I intuitively transcribed into words. I'm not sure why she referred to this dimension as "my heaven" rather than simply "heaven." Perhaps she was aware of, or had been informed that this was not her final destination. It was not the final heaven.

Most spirits exist in a celestial dimension until they are required to move onto a dimension of higher learning or to reincarnate. While in this dimension, most spirits lose their concern for earthly matters but don't completely forget the living. Some still feel a tie to their loved ones.

Group Discussion Checklist

Have you had communication with a family member in spirit?

Did the spirit of a loved one seem to have the same or a similar personality as when alive?

Has a spirit described the dimension in which it resides?

Have you experienced a heavenly dimension? Explain.

Have you had a spirit visitation when nearly asleep or in a dream state?

Changing Dimensions

After approximately thirty years, more or less, a spirit may move on to a different dimension. The thirty-year span of time before a spirit changes dimensions has been mentioned by the famous psychic Sylvia Brown on television. The approximate thirty-year span has also been confirmed twice though my communication with the spirit world.

Approximately thirty years after my mother's death, she appeared to me while in meditation. She mentally communicated to me, "I'm going to a place of higher learning. When you need me, I'll be there." I sensed my mother would know if I needed her long before I sent out a prayer or cry for help. I have since communicated with my mother many times. So it appears, in this case, even when a spirit changes dimensions, it is still able to communicate with the living.

In another instance, a young girl phoned me. She said it had been approximately thirty years since her father's death and his spirit had visited her house. She said he had notified her of his presence by sounding several notes on a music box. The music box was not wound, so under normal circumstances, it would not have played any music at all. The daughter, being psychic, sensed it was her father. She asked me to come to her house and find out why he was there. The father passed the information through automatic writing. He claimed he was required to go to another dimension. He didn't want to leave his children, but he must go. Tears came to my eyes as I sensed his emotion. Spirits have difficulty shedding tears in the next dimension, so I released his tears through my own body. It was not known why the man was sad. Perhaps he had not yet learned he would be able to return to visit his loved ones from time to time.

Many spirits remain in their assigned dimensions for approximately thirty years. The most commonly accepted hypothesis is that it takes a living person approximately thirty years after he/she reaches adulthood to set a pattern for the next generation. Therefore, those spirits have at least the next thirty years in earth time to observe the choices they had made while on earth. During that time, they may examine how their egos and free will had influenced the lives of their loved ones. The spirits may review their own mistakes or feel justified for the knowledge they had shared with their loved ones. They may make earthly visits to comfort their loved ones or influence them in positive manners. It's not known if all spirits are required to observe the consequences of previous life decisions.

After thirty years, more or less, some spirits, having observed what was necessary for their spiritual growth, may be required to enter a dimension of higher learning. This doesn't mean those spirits had learned all their lessons, or had completely understood what they observed from the living. It just means their time had run out and they must leave their current dimension, whether they want to or not. The next dimension may offer another portion of higher learning, such as spiritual growth and the true meaning of their soul's purpose. Or, the spirit may travel to, or exist in, a dimension corresponding to its spiritual awareness. The existence of in-between lives has many levels and many dimensions. It's not known how long an in-between life experience may last. It may be years or eons. Eventually, the spirit may choose to or be required to reincarnate into a physical body.

Group Discussion Checklist

Have you had a spirit visitation years after its physical death?

Do you have a book to recommend on life after death?

Discuss new knowledge.

Dimension of Lost Souls

With each class, you have become more sensitive. There will come a time just before going to sleep when you may observe the dimension of lost souls. This occurs because your brain waves have slowed down and your mind is open to infinite spiritual awareness. The dimension of lost souls is a lower dimension on the astral plane and is often observed by the novice when his or her third eye has opened for the first time. This is a dimension created by a spirit's thoughts. It is a depressing place where thousands of faces appear in the darkness, pleading for help. Many of these spirits are caught in the darkness because their thinking process is in disharmony with their selves and with the universe.

Some religions refer to this dimension as purgatory, a place of temporary punishment. However, I don't believe God created this dimension of darkness. God has an unconditional love and compassion for all humankind; therefore, it seems illogical to believe He would have created such a place of punishment. It is my belief that each person, having free will, has a mindset that shapes his or her destiny. It's up to each person to sort out what is true and what is not true. Through years of communicating with the spirit world, I have come to the conclusion that purgatory is a name that has been taught. The mind can reject or accept what it has been taught.

While observing this dark dimension, don't assume these spirits are evil just because they're in darkness. A spirit who is in disharmony with its own thoughts will find it difficult to enter its earned dimension. This may occur for a variety of reasons:

- A spirit may believe or may have been taught it's necessary to punish itself as a way to redemption.
- A spirit may cling onto a thought so fearful that it is mentally suspended in darkness.
- A spirit may fear punishment. Fear often conjures up darkness in the spirit's mind.
- A spirit may fear the unknown. It may be afraid to venture outward; therefore, it remains in the dark.
- A spirit may retain the memory of a violent life. A recent lifetime may have been so violent that the spirit is unable to release the memory; therefore, its thoughts remain suspended in the action of violence.
- A spirit could exist in a thought pattern of fear and violence for an unknown period of time.
- A spirit may hold a negative thought of guilt. It may believe it is guilty because of its recent action, or it may be a learned guilt. However, a taught guilt may or may not be by God's decree. Until the spirit understands God is unconditional compassion, the spirit's taught guilt may confine it to darkness.
- A spirit may be held in darkness simply because it's unaware of the God light. It may linger in this lower dimension until it either sees the God light or changes its thoughts away from the darkness.

I pray that in time, these spirits will become aware of the God light or of the angels who are eager to release them from their destructive states of mind. If a novice sees, in the mind's eye, a spirit in a dark dimension, he or she should not investigate it. However, if the novice wants to help, he or she may mentally direct powerful white light and positive thoughts to these pleading faces. Remember, thoughts are energy. Energy creates matter. Matter generates changes. These spirits are in darkness because they need to change their way of thinking. A novice may assist these souls by directing any positive thought that comes intuitively or mentally communicating the following message: "Go to the God light. I cannot help you at this time. Go to the God light."

The novice should mentally imagine God's light and then direct it with love toward the spirits. The novice should then mentally pass through this dimension. Notice, I sometimes refer to souls as spirits. A spirit is in darkness because its thoughts are in disharmony; therefore, it may not be aware of its true soul. But a soul that is free of earthly dogma and is in harmony with the universe is aware of its true self. The soul is free of darkness.

I'm sure there are other reasons for this dark dimension that humans have named purgatory, so I have addressed only those that I have witnessed while in meditation and the information that was communicated to me from the spirit world. I will speak only to that which I have known or sensed to be true.

Group Discussion Checklist

While in meditation or before falling asleep, have you observed or sensed a dark dimension?

Have you witnessed many faces drifting in the darkness? If so, what would you now do?

Have you previously believed a spirit in darkness was evil? What has changed your mind?

Do you believe a person can feel so unworthy that he/she can create an imaginary dark place, a purgatory, as self-punishment?

Discuss how fear or negative thoughts can confine a spirit in its own dark existence.

Darkest Dimension

While in regression, most people are not likely to observe what some refer to as hell. *Hell is not a place. It is a fatalistic thought pattern created out of fear. Hell is man's thoughts that are farthest from the consciousness of God.*

So, while down in meditation, how are you protected from this experience? An explanation is in order. Before you are regressed for a past-life reading, the God light protection had been established by the mere utterance of prayer or by the act of surrounding one's self in the light. Prayer produces light. Light is energy. Light energy is protection. Therefore, if you are seeking spiritual knowledge and enlightenment, it's not likely that you will encounter the dimension referred to as hell.

However, because we cannot comprehend all the universal laws of the spirit world, we should assume there are exceptions. An exception might be a required lesson for spiritual growth. It might be the soul's way of experiencing this hellish place for the opportunity to change one's current lifestyle to a more blessed way of living.

Hell is a man-made word used to describe the omission of God's consciousness. A spirit that is unable to see the God light might remain in any level of darkness, not necessarily a hellish dimension for a variety of reasons. Its confinement may be caused by a self-inflicted state of mind, or he/she feels a need to pay for what is a taught sin. Some people may accept the concept of man-made sin. They may believe it is a way to pay for their guilt. Also, the thought of fear may hold the spirit in the *now,* believing it should be punished for failing to lead a virtuous life. However, leading a virtuous life should come from compassion and love, not out of fear of punishment.

I don't believe God created this place man has named hell. The word *hell* may have been taught by some religions or cultures, by word of mouth, or even by parents. It is my belief that God exists in all dimensions. Yes, God is accessible even in the dark dimensions. God is absolute compassion. He understands man's struggle. Therefore, it does not seem logical that God would have created such a place as purgatory or hell.

Group Discussion Checklist

Do you believe God is absolute compassion and love?

How can a belief create the concept of hell or purgatory?

How can a near-death experience of a hellish dimension change one's lifestyle?

How can a near-death experience of heaven change one's lifestyle?

How can fear take control of a person's thoughts?

How does fear affect the mind or physical body?

Have you ever lived in fear for a short time and then realized how fear had kept you from proceeding in your daily life?

Please check your personal list. Have you deleted any issues?

In-Between-Life Dimension

While you are in meditation or regression to view a past live and if you have the ability to lower your brain waves to theta or delta, you may be fortunate enough to experience an in-between-life dimension. This is a rare experience. There are many different dimensions in the world beyond. An in-between life may appear as a place of absolute peace, universal harmony, and awe-inspiring beauty. While viewing this dimension, you might see endless waves of colorful vibrations, feel a heavenly serenity, or just observe an endless space filled with emotion rather than words. The recall may last a few seconds, rarely minutes, but may encompass thousands of years. While in this dimension, you may not want to speak or answer questions. If so, raise your hand to silence the group while observing this divine dimension.

Group Discussion Checklist

Have you experienced an in-between-life dimension? Explain.

While in meditation, have you observed or sensed the peace and harmony of another dimension?

Explain your definition of "complete serenity." Not everyone's answer will be the same. Your interpretation will change as awareness grows.

Dimension of Absolute Harmony

When reviewing a past life or while down in meditation, you may observe what I have named the "Dimension of Universal Harmony." However, you may name this dimension anything you believe it means to you. This dimension gives evidence that humans are multidimensional beings and are connected to the All. When your mind is existing in the now of this dimension, you may receive an astute awareness of the surroundings. One of the many things you may see within your mind's eye are rows of pale rainbows moving slowly through an endless void of darkness and space. Each color, each hue, even each space between the colors is emitting different wavelengths of vibrations. Humans may perceive this phenomenon as a musical scale of rainbows. It is the way people convert symbols into a meaning. While viewing this dimension, you will become aware you are a part of this colorful rainbow and a part of billions and billions of souls harmoniously joined together. You may feel you are a part of a continuous stream of souls moving slowly through universal space. If you wish to remain longer in this dimension, raise your hand to stop all outside communication and remain in a deep state of awareness.

I have experienced the dimension of absolute harmony as follows: While in meditation, I observed a beautiful rainbow so wide that it extended past my visual concept of distance. That rainbow stretched out ahead and behind me as far as I could see. As I, my soul, drifted slowly through space, I became aware that I was a part of the rainbow. I was not a body. I had no awareness of arms or legs. I was a soul of pure mind, aware of the all of the universe. The colors of the rainbow varied from delicate pale hues of pink to vibrant purple colors. Each color represented a note on the musical scale. I sensed each note as it vibrated. I didn't hear the actual sound; I understood the sound. I was aware that each sound was in perfect harmony with the rainbow. As I drifted peacefully along, I became aware that each sound was sending out delicate waves of vibrations. I saw the vibrations as ripples in an ocean. The vibrations spread out beyond my visual perception. I realized each color and vibration was in perfect harmony with the universe.

While in this dimension, I recognized myself as being a part of God; a part of the rainbow; a part of all energy; a part of all souls; a part of all things, animate and inanimate, living and in spirit; a part of the All. I became aware the colors of the rainbow were connected to everything and extended in all directions. I knew, as an absolute truth, I was experiencing an accumulation of souls in absolute harmony within the universe.

I sensed my love as a part of myself spreading out toward the earth below. As I, my soul, connected with the earth, I became aware that I was a part of each cloud, each breeze, each raindrop. I drifted closer to the earth. I became a part of the earth, a part of each tree and each blade of grass. I drifted closer. I merged into each living plant, each living creature, and finally into each living human being. I was a part of all earthly people. I was a part of the All.

This Dimension of Absolute Harmony did not stop at the earth. I sensed my soul spreading outward like the melodious sound of heavenly harps, heading toward each planet in the solar system. I intuitively knew that I had once been a part of each planet, because I was familiar with their energy. The realization of the solar system did not end here. I witnessed billions upon trillions of stars, and I knew that I was connected to each in a personal, loving way.

My soul expanded past the end of the universes. I was witnessing the primordial soup of the universes swirling before the beginning of time. This swirling motion whirls into infinity. I was witnessing the creation of the universes. I understood, as this was occurring, I was in the now of the creation, and it is still occurring. I realized that I had been there from the very beginning. I was connected to God, to the All. This whole experience was instantaneous and complete, and it encompassed an ageless measure of time. This regression had taken only several minutes, yet the entire harmony of the universe had been revealed to me.

Humans separate time in minutes, days, years, and so on. Time is different on the other side. What may take a lifetime for humans to experience may take only a matter of seconds to experience on the other side. That's why I was able to see and experience so much in so little time. It's fortunate when one is able to witness all or a part of the sacred Dimension of Absolute Harmony. It's an inspiration to be more harmonious in life. Those who are spiritually aware will recognize the spiritual beauty of its pure harmony. They will recognize all people are connected to God; therefore, all people are connected.

Group Discussion Checklist

While in meditation or regression, have you viewed a dimension similar to the Dimension of Absolute Harmony?

Have you ever sensed or felt the emotion of absolute harmony?

Does the Dimension of Absolute Harmony give a clearer explanation of how man is connected to God and the universe?

Have you learned to remain in the *now* of peaceful harmony when life becomes stressful?

How would you explain the feeling of *being in the now* of absolute harmony?

Eye of God

It's rare but possible while down in meditation to observe the eye of God. The eye may appear as small as a teacup or larger than a room. It may appear as a brilliant light. Some may not see the image but only sense the supreme compassion of the God consciousness or whomever they honor as the supreme being. This is an awe-inspiring experience, and it will not be easily forgotten. There are many other celestial dimensions one might view, each serene, tranquil, and usually lasting only seconds. Celestial dimensions may be observed while in regression, viewing a past life, during meditation, or just before falling asleep.

Listed above are only several of the many dimensions that I have experienced. I have named them according to my own interpretation of the dimension. Each person may experience different dimensions, and he/she may name them according to his or her personal experience. Each soul has a journey, a life path to travel, a lesson to learn, and perhaps an unusual spiritual experience to encounter.

Group Discussion Checklist

What information did you find most interesting and useful?

Have you or will you ask your angels or guides to show you a dimension that will be of value in this lifetime?

Have you experienced a celestial dimension? Explain.

Review your personal list. What new information has helped release fears?

Exercise. Past-Life Reading

A past-life regression requires two people, the director and the reader. For this exercise, we will use the term *he* for the director and *she* for the reader. This exercise is best performed when the reader is lying down so the body can relax more easily. The deeper the relaxation, the keener the awareness. When the brain waves have slowed down, the pulse, heart, and all bodily functions have also slowed down. At this time, the reader may become acutely sensitive to atmospheric changes. She may detect a cold or icy area over her body or detect a spirit's presence as a slight breeze or an icy chill. She may also sense or feel the cool presence of angels or guides who are assisting in the reading. Therefore, she may wish to cover herself with a blanket while the reading is in progress.

Humans and spirits vibrate at different rates of speed. Human vibrations are moving energy. Spirits vibrate faster than humans do. Guides vibrate faster than spirits. Angels vibrate faster than guides. Angels vibrate extremely fast because their essence is of a finer ethereal essence. The finer the vibration, the less likely humans can detect its angelic presence. Archangels are powerful, and they vibrate extremely fast; therefore, they are seldom seen by the human eye.

Preparation to a Past-Life Reading

It is each member's responsibility to see that no imbalanced or negative person joins the group. Negative energy will siphon the positive energy, making it difficult for the reader to see within the mind's eye. An imbalanced person could draw like-minded spirits or energy toward the group. Like draws like. Maintain your group with a high spiritual intention.

As stated above, a past-life reading requires two people, the director and the reader. A third person may assist by taking notes or monitoring a recording device. Other members may listen in, but must not interfere with the reading. Each group will select a private corner of the room. All telephones should be turned off. The lights are dimmed to allow the reader to see within the mind's eye more easily. It's important not to eat a heavy meal before the reading. For best results, don't eat red meat the day of the reading, as the body may still be processing food that will distract from complete concentration. Do not smoke as it may obstruct another reader's ability to breathe deeply. Absolutely no alcohol before class. The mind must be clear and responsive to the experience. The voice should be lowered to a whisper during the reading so it does not disturb other readers.

Select your partner intuitively. It's best to select a different partner for each regression until you find the one person who connects best with you. As each past life is recalled, some past lives may seem ordinary and uninteresting at first glance. Be patient and stay in the moment to observe the past life. Discover who you were and what lessons had been learned during that lifetime. When observing an interesting past life, remain calm, hold your hand up, motioning for the director to halt any outside communication momentarily, and then enjoy the scene of the moment.

A past-life regression is most rewarding when we can face ourselves, who we were, and what we had done in the past. Most importantly, we should recognize how we have changed since our last incarnation. As we observe what had occurred in the past, we will be better equipped to release the negative memories that have caused fears, phobias, or psychosomatic illnesses in this present life.

The Director

The director has the responsibility to see that no person touches or startles the reader while she is regressed. When the reader is completely relaxed, the director will request a past-life memory to come forward. He should watch for rapid eye movement (REM), indicating the reader is viewing a scene. During rapid eye movement, he should give the reader time to experience the scene before asking a question. The director should encourage the reader to speak of what she is seeing in her mind's eyes. He should not ask mixed questions or interrupt the reader. He may use his own phrases or repeat any of the following suggestions:

- "Feel yourself going back in time. Back to a lifetime important to this soul's development."
- "Going back ... back ... several centuries. Deeper and deeper. Your guides will assist you."
- "Go back to a lifetime when this soul was with (name a specific person)."
- "Going back to a time when a great lesson was learned that would benefit this soul at this time."
- "Allow your guides to take you back to a lifetime that will benefit your spiritual development."
- "Drifting back in time until an important event occurs."
- "Visualize a calendar. See the calendar going back in time. What is the year or date on a calendar?"

The director must have the knowledge and ability to notice if the reader is having difficulty with a specific past life. If a death scene or traumatic scene presents itself, the director must coach the reader through the trauma by saying, "You are rising above the scene. You are only observing. You are only observing."

If the reader still appears distressed, the director should coach the reader to observe the trauma by using a repetition of any or all of the following statements:

- "You are rising above the scene."
- "You do not feel pain."
- "You are not connected to this scene."
- "You are only watching."
- "You are no longer connected to that life."
- "You are only observing."

If the reader appears to be having difficulty separating herself from the scene, the director should count her up to the present time as follows: "You are coming back. You are no longer connected to that life. You are releasing *this* memory. You are releasing. Coming back to the present time. Feeling very, very good. Coming back. On the count of three, your eyes will open. One. Two. Three."

Or the director may use any method or words that are intuitively received.

The Reader

Before going down in regression, the reader may advise the director what she wants to experience. Or the reader may, on mental suggestion, direct her mind to recall a past life or a specific era in time. The reader will close her eyes and listen to the director as he talks her down to a deeper level of meditation. She may mentally use any of the following suggestions:

- Mentally say, "I call upon my guides and angels for protection and guidance."
- Mentally request of her guides or angels, "Take me to a specific time or place."
- Mentally request of her guides, "Take me to an important past life that will benefit my present life."
- Mentally request, "Take me back to a time when I was with (name a specific person)."

- If the reader feels the director is taking her down too fast, tell him to slow down.
- If the reader feels she is not at a deep enough level of awareness, let the director know.
- If the reader feels the director is asking too many questions, raise the hand to halt the questions.
- If the reader senses a specific lifetime is not important, or for any reason she cannot, or does not, want to continue with this particular past life, say so.
- As images appear in the mind's eye, the reader may look into the eyes of that image for recognition. A past life can be recognized by looking into the eyes for the soul. The body may be different, but the soul remains the same. The reader may recognize a present-life family member or friend by the soul within the eyes of a past-life entity.
- Explain to the director what she is seeing or sensing.
- Mentally ask the past-life entities questions. Suggest the entities motion by shaking their head from side to side for no, or up and down, for yes.
- Describe the clothing, scenery, country, nationality, emotion, date, year, or season.
- Visualize the calendar for the date or year of the past life.

After the reading is done, the reader should release any negative aspect of that past-life memory. Send the negativity to the God light, where it will be transmuted to light. Then mentally count herself up from three to one. Or she may wait for the director to count her back. After the reading has been accomplished, she may discuss her experience in a whisper. Do not to disturb the other readers.

The director and the group will remain seated during the following meditation. The reader should be lying down, ready to be further regressed. The group will then go down into meditation.

Meditation to Recall a Past-Life Memory

"Close your eyes. Visualize a cloud of white light. God is light. God is love. Slowly ... deeply ... breathing in the white light. The light is wrapping around your body. God is light. God is love. This is your God light protection. (Pause.) Your forehead is relaxing. Feel the relaxation going down your face. Your jaw is relaxing. (Pause.) Your eyes are relaxing. Slowly take a deep breath and hold it as long as is comfortable. As you exhale, your neck is relaxing. (Pause.) Feel the relaxation going down your shoulders … down your arms. Your hands are relaxing. Slowly take a deep breath and hold it as long as is comfortable. You're breathing slowly … deeply. Relaxing … relaxing … relaxing. (Pause.) Your forehead is relaxing. Your eyes are relaxing. Becoming pure mind. Knowing exactly where you are at all times. Knowing exactly what you're doing. Going deeper and deeper in awareness. Becoming pure mind. Concentrate on your third eye.

"You're going back in time. Drifting back to another lifetime … another place. Mentally ask your guides for protection, guidance, and information. Feeling very … peaceful. You're drifting back in time."

*End of meditation.

Begin exercise to past-live regression.

The director and the group will open their eyes. The reader will remain in a deep state of mediation. The director should mentally place white-light protection around himself and the reader. He may use any introduction intuitively received or repeat any part of the following: "Slowly take a deep breath and hold it as long as comfortable. Slowly exhaling. Feel yourself relaxing … relaxing. Going deeper … and deeper … into awareness. You're breathing slowly … deeply. Going back … in time. Drifting back … back … back in time."

Begin reading. The reading may last ten to thirty minutes or as long as agreed upon. After the reading is completed, the director may repeat the following meditation in a soft, monotone voice.

Meditation to Return from a Past-Life Regression

"Coming back to the present time. Your breathing is getting deeper … stronger. Coming back. Slowly take a deep breath. Your breathing is getting deeper … stronger. On the count of three, you will open your eyes, feeling very, very good. Coming back. One … two … three. Open your eyes."

*End of meditation.

Or the director or the reader may use any method they receive intuitively.

Group Discussion Checklist

Did you feel your mind or body drifting back in time?

What, if any, past life did you experience?

Did you sense you had once lived a specific life before it was revealed in regression?

What, if any, lessons were learned from a past life?

Did the scene appear in color or black and white?

Did you observe a style of clothing you had never seen before? Or was the clothing familiar?

Did you recognize a person in your present life by the soul within the eyes?

Did you face or release a fear?

Did your past life explain any talents, fears, or phobias?

Do you now understand why a certain person or place is important to you in this present life?

Chapter 11
AUTOMATIC WRITING

Automatic writing is a method by which the human mind can receive information at different levels of awareness. The mind is like a computer. It can draw upon information from the conscious mind, subconscious mind, super-subconscious mind, or a spirit's mind. A writer who is spiritually aware will reach a more meaningful level of awareness than a novice. The message is usually communicated to the writer by thought transference or by a spirit moving the writer's hand.

For this exercise, the writer will be known as she. The writer will take several deep breaths to slow down her brain waves to alpha. This will activate the intuitive (right) side of the brain. The eyes may be open or closed. When the eyes are closed, the writer is able to tune into the intuitive side of the brain more easily because she is not distracted by outside events. As the writer's ability improves, the eyes may remain open for longer periods of time while writing. Try both ways to find which method is best for you. A paranormal experience, such as automatic writing, is an unproven science coming from an extrasensory point of view. The method will change depending upon the writer's progress or the importance of the information being received. Automatic writing is usually done by the hand, but a typewriter or computer can be used. The writer may receive information by different methods. For example:

- The writer may tune into the intuitive right brain and then record the information on the paper.

- A spirit or spirit guide may influence the writer's thoughts. The writer will write the message as she is mentally receiving it.
- A spirit or spirit guide may direct the writer's hand. She should let the hand move freely. She should not allow outside thoughts to interfere or color the message she is receiving.

Because a writer may be contacting different spirits, she should begin each writing by mentally asking for the "very highest spiritual guidance I am capable of using." The writer should then mentally wrap herself in a circle of white light or call upon her angels and guides for protection and guidance.

Automatic writing should not be attempted until all previous exercises have been completed and the writer has a clear understanding of the spirit world. She must be able to sense whether the thought entering her brain or the energy moving her hand feels like a positive or a negative force. She must recognize a negative energy quickly so she can prevent it from influencing the writing.

The writer is using the intuitive (right) side of the brain when writing. The right side of the brain receives information through emotion, while the left side of the brain uses logic. Often, the information comes through very fast. The first thing a novice writer will notice is a verb is often placed before a noun, and the sentence does not have proper punctuation. This occurs because the right side of the brain is receiving information by symbols, emotion, or sensing. Don't stop writing to correct the spelling, punctuation, or sentence structure. If the writing is scribbled or the sentences read illogically, stay with it while the writing is flowing. The left side of the brain, the logic brain, will kick in when needed. It will make the necessary corrections when the writing is done for the day.

Group Discussion Checklist

Do you sometimes write fast and forget to place the nouns and verbs in proper order? If so, you may be receiving information from the intuitive right side of the brain or from a spirit.

Do ideas pop into your head while writing?

When to Write

The writer should write when alone or when she is not likely to be disturbed. Write late in the evening when there is less interference from a telephone, radio, family, or company. If the writer wishes to become an accomplished automatic writer, she should mentally convey that desire to her personal guides. She should set a specific time of day when she will write. She should not write sporadically and expect a guide to wait around until she calls upon them for assistance. Guides have other meaningful duties. If the writer is consistent and sincere, the guides will see and read the message in her aura light. She must keep the value of her questions on a high level so the guides will be willing to assist.

Changes in Script

A novice's first attempt at automatic writing may be illegible scribbles or large jumbled print. Automatic writing is usually written in the writer's handwriting. However, when a spirit enters the writer's energy field (aura), a change of script may appear. The writing may flow as large scrolling letters, boxlike and square print, curvy and flowing letters, or faint and small print. The script will usually reveal the personality of the writer's contact.

Large boxy print may indicate a bold, assertive spirit is assisting in the writing. Or it may be a spirit who prefers to print rather than write cursive. Small or faint print may indicate a timid, hesitant spirit. Each form of print will identify the spirit who is assisting that day. The size and appearance of the script will change from time to time, indicating a different spirit is moving in and out of the writer's energy field.

When I first began automatic writing, the script was composed of oddly phrased sentences with archaic or ancient words. It was a form of script I had never known but produced without effort. To me, this indicated a very ancient spirit was directing my automatic writing. I surmised it was a spiritual master by the peaceful, compassionate feeling that had entered my body and by the ancient words used to communicate the information. At that time, these highly evolved masters introduced concepts beyond my comprehension. I saved many writings. It was at least ten years before I realized that the messages contained valuable information that I now understand. Therefore, if an unusual form of script continues for several months, the writer might assume it is her personal guide, a master spirit, or a spirit communicating the messages. With practice, the writer will learn to recognize her personal guide or the script writer by the penmanship and the words used.

Group Discussion Checklist

Have you sensed an answer as you are writing?

Does your writing change from large print to small cursive? Explain.

Have you felt someone was assisting you in thought or writing?

Sources of Automatic Writing

The writer may receive information from different sources. The source reached will depend upon the writer's spiritual awareness and psychic ability. Information can come from the highest dimension, the God consciousness, or from a lower dimension of mischievous spirits. I will speak only to those who are familiar to me. But keep in mind there are more communicators than those listed below.

The **conscious mind** is a source of information. It contains what a person has learned, thinks, or consciously knows in this present life. It relates to taste, touch, smell, sight, and sound. It directs one's daily actions. The conscious mind uses both sides of the brain, the logical left brain and the intuitive right brain. The writer's logical left brain may influence the automatic writing according to the way the writer envisions herself. Logic often colors one's writing, thus invalidating part of the message received in automatic writing. Therefore, the writer should not use logic. She should only accept what is intuitively received.

Group Discussion Checklist

Explain what you understand about the conscious mind.

Explain the conscious mind as it relates to taste, touch, smell, sight, and sound.

The **subconscious mind** is another source of information. The mind is like a computer, storing vast amounts of memory and knowledge. With meditation and training, the writer can learn to draw information from the subconscious mind and record it through automatic writing.

Finding a lost article would be an example. The subconscious mind is aware of where the article was placed (lost). The writer need only slow down her brain waves and then mentally call upon the subconscious mind to write the location of the lost article.

The subconscious mind contains cell memories from the writer's present and past lives. The writer may also have inherited some cell memories from her ancestor's, dating back to unknown periods of time. Some of these cell memories may be memorable enough to have affected the writer's present-day point of view. Recalling a past life can be revealed through automatic writing, especially if the writer is sincere and the information is intended to strengthen the writer's spiritual awareness.

Group Discussion Checklist
Explain how the conscious mind differs from the subconscious mind.

The **intuitive mind** senses information during automatic writing. It may sense or see images and symbols in the mind's eye. It may receive messages from different sources, such as spirit guides or an unknown spirit. In automatic writing, the intuitive right side of the brain is used to receive information, while the logical left side of the brain is less active.

Group Discussion Checklist
Do you receive information intuitively? Explain.
Do you know from whom you are receiving information?

Personal spirit guides are the most common source of information used in automatic writing. The writer may ask the name of her personal guides. If the writer knows the name of her personal guides, she may ask them to identify themselves each time she writes. Or she may ask them to begin all writings with the same key phrase. As the writer becomes familiar with her guides' script, she will feel confident of the message received. Personal guides often give information for the writer's spiritual development.

Information may also come from another person's personal guide. Personal guides are able to transfer information back and forth by thought. Another person's guide may contact your personal guide, who will then mentally transfer the information to you, the writer.

Group Discussion Checklist
Are you aware of your personal guides? Explain?
Do you feel you have been helped by your personal guides?
Do you ask for help from your personal guides?
Explain different ways your personal guides can offer assistance.

Any **spirit guide** may enter the writer's energy field (aura) to write a message. It may communicate its message mentally or use its energy to move the writer's hand. If the writer has a specific talent, spirit guides who have an expertise in that field can inspire the writer to further develop that talent. Spirits guides are eager to offer assistance and to pass on knowledge. The writer can mentally ask a spirit guide for assistance in most matters. The spirit guide will enter the writer's aura to communicate the answer or inspire creativity. Because there are many spirits, there are also many spirits who possess an expertise in medical, mechanical, office work, politics, sewing or any craft, etc.

Any **spirit** may communicate a message through automatic writing. The hand will move as the spirit's thoughts pass through the writer's brain. It's similar to writing a letter. The writer thinks the words and then writes the words. It's as simple as that. However, just because it's easy to write words that come to mind doesn't mean those words are accurate. The automatic writing will depend upon the writer's sincerity and spiritual awareness.

Spirits *want* to be asked. Angels *need t*o be asked. *Ask, and ye shall receive.*

Spirits communicate by thought. The writer should be sure from whom the words have originated. She must recognize if the spirit relaying the message is of white light, therefore offering accurate information, or if the spirit is of darkness and will threaten or attempt to scare the writer. The writer usually feels confident when the writing is accurate but hesitant when the writing is not accurate.

Sometimes the hand will move without the writer receiving any mental communication. This may occur when a spirit moves the writer's hand to convey a message. Because the writer doesn't sense the messenger, it may be difficult to recognize whether it has positive or negative energy. Therefore, it's important to begin automatic writing with a prayer or by covering one's self in white light.

Group Discussion Checklist
How do you recognize a negative feeling from a positive feeling?
What would you do if a spirit threatens you while writing?
Discuss the phrase, "Spirits *want* to be asked. Angels *need t*o be asked. *Ask, and ye shall receive.*"

Spirits can make their presence known by a light touch as gentle as a feather touching the human body. Some spirits can be felt as a cold chill. The cold feeling is the spirit vibrating at a different rate of speed than a human, or the spirit may be absorbing energy from the atmosphere.

Most spirits can only frighten the living. However, a fearful person may react with a cold sweat or a rapid heartbeat. Sometimes a rash or welts may appear on the person's body. It is not always the spirit that is causing the problem. Sometimes it is the living person's own fear that causes the rash or welt to appear. Under some circumstances, a spirit can move an object or touch a living person, but rarely does it cause harm to the living.

If the writer is using automatic writing for an improper purpose, this could draw like-minded spirits. A negative writer who emits a negative aura may unwittingly draw negative spirits toward him/her. If the writer attempts to meddle in someone's personal affairs, this could cause like-minded spirits to slip into the writer's energy field. The quality of writing will be affected. Like draws like. Negativity opens the doorway to negative interferences. Therefore, the writer must be able to recognize negative spirits, and he/she must be able to block the spirit's entrance into his or her energy field.

The **higher self (the soul)** may give information while writing. This is a part of the super-subconscious mind that understands the universal law. It identifies with the unity of all creation. Contact with this level depends upon the writer's spiritual awareness and the purity of intentions at the time of the writing. This may require the writer to slow down the brain waves to alpha or lower. However, even at this level of awareness, if the writer is a novice, he/she may not fully understand all the information in the message. It may be too advanced to grasp at this time. The writer should record the message and save it for a later time when he/she is ready to understand its meaning.

The **Universal Consciousness, Akashic Records, and God Wisdom** are the highest sources of spiritual intelligence. They are the trinity aspect of the same God energy. The universal consciousness holds all knowledge available to the person's soul, whether psychic or not. The Akashic Records are imprinted knowledge in and of the universes. The God wisdom consists of all universal wisdom.

The trinity levels of awareness require the writer to maintain a deep meditative state of mind. These aspects of God are not usually or easily accessed through automatic writing. However, if the writer is fortunate enough to come in contact with the trinity aspect, he or she may sense the spirit's wisdom as a compassionate feeling, or his or her body will feel compacted with love and/or feel extremely large in size. This will confirm that message is coming from an angelic or celestial being.

Edgar Cayce was thought to have accessed the Akashic Records. Cayce was born in 1877 and died 1945. He resided in Virginia Beach, Virginia, and is known as America's most documented psychic. Many of Cayce's books refer to his health reading. While Cayce was in a deep meditative trance, it was believed that he received information from the Akashic Records. He would lie down, close his eyes, and enter a consciousness like the Akashic Records. He would then tune into a client only by name. The client could have been hundreds or thousands of miles away. He would reveal the client's present-day illness and a healing or cure for that illness. Sometimes he would reveal a client's past life experience that involved a specific illness.

The **Akashic Records** are not usually available to the novice writer. Of course, there are always exceptions to the rule. It is rare but possible to access a divine dimension if the writer is truly sincere and spiritually motivated. Sincerity is the door to extrasensory perception (ESP). A spiritual message may be communicated to the writer by thought transference, and because a divine dimension is farthest from an earthly dimension, it will be a mental communication. Therefore, a divine spiritual reading may not involve physical contact to the writer's hand or a spirit entering the writer's aura. The writer is to write the words as the thoughts come into his or her head.

Group Discussion Checklist

What past-life experiences do you believe have influenced your present-day point of view?

What do you understand about the subconscious mind? This knowledge will change as spiritual development grows.

Archangels and **angels** don't usually convey information through automatic writing. They can, but they don't transmit information in the same way as guides do. An angel may transmit information to the writer's spirit guide. The writer's spirit guide will then relay the information to the writer's mind. Automatic writing comes through the human mind, while angels come through the heart. That is why when an archangel or spiritual master is near, the physical body can feel its presence as unconditional love and compassion.

All spiritual messages come from one source—**God.** Archangels, angels, and spirit guides are all one, but on different levels of spiritual awareness. They don't separate one from the other, because they know we are all *one*. Angels and archangels do give information, but it is usually subscribed through spirit guides or spirits. An angel's energy is so very powerful that the writer would find it difficult to accept its energy into his or her mind or energy field.

I have personally experienced the immense power of archangels, angels, and spirit guides many times. I have physically felt the angel's power as a bolt of lightning and a trembling of thunder surging through my body as they assisted me in rescuing an earthbound spirit. The force was so powerful it actually tightened the muscles in my left leg. Several days later, I had to go to a chiropractor to release the muscle in my leg. Other than that, I felt extremely well and happy after the encounter. An angel may come without notice or invitation. It is the angel's choice.

On several occasions, I have experienced an angel enter my body without the forceful jolt or surge of power. Therefore, I surmised an angel is able to temper its power before coming close to or entering the human aura or body. I have also experienced an angel enter my body to give a blessing to a class that I was teaching. As the angel entered my body, I felt huge and that my body had extended over and beyond the house. This angel transmitted the feeling of wisdom in the form of absolute love and compassion for all humankind. I felt honored to have experienced the power and love of an angel.

There are many other reasons why an angel does not usually come in direct contact with humans in the same way as spirit guides or spirits do. Therefore, I will only speak to that which I have learned from personal experiences.

Group Discussion Checklist
Have you been helped or rescued from danger by an angel?
What does the angel mean by "We are all one?"
What, if any, contact or experiences have you had with an angel?
Have you experienced the power of an angel?
Have you seen or sensed an angel?
Share your knowledge of an angel.
Recommend a book on angels.

Positive Attitude
The writer should truly believe she can receive information through automatic writing. Believing in one's self sends a positive energy into the ethereal. Angels and guides see and read the aura energy. Many years ago, I received the following information from my guide, describing the importance of a positive attitude. It is written exactly as it was mentally received: "So should you dwell on the positive fact, *it will be done*. That which you learn to accept *will be so*. That which you truly believe is so, *then it is so*. If you think it is so, it may not be so. But if you know it is so, *so shall it be*. That is the creation of life."

Group Discussion Checklist
Discuss the spirit's message.
Discuss the difference between believe, think, and know.
Check your personal list for any new changes.

Writing Guides
If the writer is sincere about receiving information through automatic writing, he/she may be assigned a writing guide by the spiritual realm. The writer may call upon a writing guide at work or to assist in writing a short article, a manuscript, or even a play. Writing guides have been known to assist authors in writing books. They are often referred to as muses. Writing guides may once have been famous writers who lived many years ago, or they may be unknown spirit writers who are eager

to share their expertise. Remember, spirit guides are here to guide and inspire you, not serve you.

Group Discussion Checklist

Do you have a talent or expertise that needs assistance from a spirit guides?

Do you feel inspired to a specific talent, hobby, or writing style?

Have you recognized when a guide has or is assisting you?

Have you been puzzled, unable to finish a project, when suddenly the answer comes out of the blue?

Do you recognize when you are begin helped by a spirit?

Name several daily chores where a spirit guide can assist.

Will you now call upon a guide for knowledge or assistance more often?

Mischievous Spirits

A mischievous spirit may slip into the writer's energy field (aura) to communicate false information. It may attempt to threaten, frighten, or interrupt the novice writer. Some spirits are not guides, and sometimes the writer doesn't know which spirit is influencing the writing. If the novice writer becomes frightened, his or her aura will emit a negative energy. A playful spirit may try to frighten the writer for the sole purpose of siphoning aura energy. This loss of aura energy does not harm the writer because aura energy is naturally being discharged daily, whether a spirit absorbs the energy or not.

Meddling Spirits

Meddling spirits may attempt to influence the writer's thoughts. Some spirits still have an emotional tie to earth and are not ready to cross over into the God light. Some spirits are earthbound through lack of knowledge, unaware of the God light, or bound to the earthly dimension for a variety of reasons. Meddling spirits enjoy playful interaction with humans. They may move or hide an object, ring a telephone, or knock on the door, but they are not evil. They mean no harm. They are just interacting with us for their own entertainment. Sometimes it appears they are trying to frighten us, but usually, they are just trying to get our attention. Some spirits simply need help or guidance.

Just because spirits are meddlesome doesn't mean they are evil. Frightened spirits often appear evil. The writer may sense their fear, frustration, or anger, and mistake them as evil. However, in truth, most earthbound spirits are scared because they don't know what to do.

If a negative spirit intrudes upon a writing, the writer has the right and the power to ask the angels or guides to politely (or with force) send it away. A personal guide may mentally instruct the writer on how to handle a mischievous spirit. The writer may use any of the following phrases:

- "Stand back."
- "Go to the God light."
- "None shall enter (the writer's aura) but love."

These phrases, with the help of the guide and God's light, will send a bothersome spirit on its way. The power of the God light is immense. It will set a negative spirit aside. There are many phrases that will set a negative spirit aside. Each person will learn to use information he/she intuitively receives.

Group Discussion Checklist

Have you encountered a mischievous spirit?

Have you ever been wakened from a deep sleep by what sounded like the doorbell or phone ringing?

Have you heard rapping or knocking?

Have objects been moved or hidden in your purse, wallet, or home?

Do you recognize when an object has been moved by a spirit? Pay attention. It happens more often than you realize.

Contact a Deceased Loved One

The writer may contact a deceased person through automatic writing. The writer may mentally request or write the name of the person whom he/she wishes to contact. The writer will hold an object that once belonged to the deceased to intensify the energy. The deceased person can see the request flowing from the writer's aura and may be drawn toward the aura energy. The deceased may not answer on the first try. It may need time to learn how to enter the earthly dimension just as the writer is learning how to tune into the spirit's dimension. Eventually, either the deceased or a personal guide will answer the message. Don't be discouraged. Some spirits choose not to answer at all.

Exercise. Automatic Writing

The group will mentally place a circle of white light around their bodies for protection. Any prayer of protection may be prayed, or the following prayer may be used: "I ask the God light for protection and guidance. I ask this information come from the highest spiritual guidance I am capable of using at this time."

Sit erect to keep the spine straight. Don't cross the legs at the knees, as this will twist the spine and interrupt the natural flow of energy through the body. Hold the pencil upright with the lead lightly touching the paper. Neither the hand nor the wrist should touch the paper. The hand must be able to move freely across the paper. If a novice needs extra energy to begin writing, a person may stand behind the writer and place his or her hands on the writer's shoulders to transfer energy to the writer. The person will breathe in, drawing the universal energy into his or her body, direct it through the body, and then send the energy into the writer. This energy will then be used by the writer.

The writer should breathe in deeply and then exhale slowly. This will allow the mind and body to quiet down. The eyes may be open or closed as the writer mentally or verbally asks a question. Information will be received as a series of thoughts without the conscious use of logic or by the automatic movement of the hand. If the hand does not move, the writer may encourage movement by drawing a continuous flow of circles. Be patient. Expect the first writings to be large, scribbled, printed, or unsteady. It may take time for the attending spirit to learn to direct the writer's hand or to put thoughts into the writer's mind.

Here are some suggested questions for beginners to ask:

- Are you my guide?
- How can I help you? How can you help me?
- What is your name?
- How long have you been my guide? Years? Lifetimes?
- How will I recognize my personal guide when writing?
- What is my spiritual path?

The writer should mentally ask one question at a time. Wait until each question is completely answered before going onto the next question. Be patient until the complete message has come through. To avoid a mixed or confusing answer, don't combine two questions. Keep each question clear so there is no possibility of misinterpretation by either the writer or the assisting spirit.

Begin meditation. Begin writing.

Group Discussion Checklist
Did you receive a message by thought?
Did your hand move on its own?
Did you close your eyes occasionally to retain the alpha level?
Did you sense the answer before you wrote it?
Did you learn the name of your personal guide?
Was there a change in emotion or feeling when a different spirit entered your energy field?
Was there a change in script?
What, if any, information did you receive?
Did you remember to thank your guides and angels?
Check your personal list. Have you reconciled any questionable issues through automatic writing?

The Bursting Light-bulb

When something unusual happens, we often overlook it as an accident or quirk of nature. However, if we look more closely, we discover the mystery of the universe is hidden within such unusual happenings. The Bursting Light-bulb is a true story that illustrates the power drawn in when using automatic writing.

The event that convinced me of the value of automatic writing came one cold winter evening. I had waited until the evening sun had set before sitting down to write. It was my habit to sit in a comfortable chair with an artist's canvas board on my lap to hold the paper. Once I was sure I would be comfortable enough to write a long time, I turned on the lamp beside me, lowered my brain waves, and prepared to receive information. As I began to write, I noticed my cat, Misty, had entered the family room and had sat down in front of me. The cat seemed to be deeply engrossed in watching something just above my left hand, the hand that was holding the pencil. Half an hour went by. The cat sat motionless, watching with a curious expression on its face. I closed my eyes to see in my mind's eye and checked the spot where the cat was staring. I sensed a ball of energy hovering over my left hand. I am left-handed and always write with the left hand. I didn't actually see the energy. I sensed it. So I wasn't sure if that was what the cat was watching. Every once in a while, I would glance down at the cat. He seemed to be curiously amused and never took his eyes off my writing hand.

Suddenly, the silence of my meditative mood was broken when the light-bulb in the lamp next to me shattered, scattering glass over the table, chair, and floor. The cat jumped up and dashed out of the room. I jumped up, too, as thin shards of glass flew across my writing board. I checked my face and hands. Somehow, I had remained untouched.

I set aside the writing, wiped up the fine shards of glass, and replaced the light-bulb. When I settled down to write again, it suddenly dawned on me: Why not ask why the light-bulb burst? Even as I considered the question, my hand began to race across the paper. The pen pressed down firmly, and the message came in large, bold print: "We come in great numbers. We are pleased that you have chosen to use this information. The glass bulb shattered because our energy is great. Continue writing."

As I finished the last sentence, I became aware of a fullness in the room that I had not noticed before. *So this is what a room full of spirits feels like,* I thought. The full feeling that encompassed the room was peacefully and pleasantly energetic. When something so out-of-the-ordinary like this happens, it confirms the mysterious energies of the universe. It encouraged me that I was on the right track. The shattering of the light-bulb, the presence of many spirits, and the powerful message reassured me I was receiving messages from sources other than my own imagination.

However, there were also days when the pencil would not move at all. I would sit patiently for a long time before asking, "Why won't the pencil move?" But the pencil would remain still. On those days, I became aware the room seemed empty, void of energy. I learned to cancel the writing because on those days, either a friend would ask to meet me or the telephone would ring and would have interrupted my writing anyway. I came to realize the guides had known these interruptions would occur long before I had, and they had canceled the session before it begun.

Questions Answered through Automatic Writing

The following information is only a small portion of the messages I have received over the course of nearly forty years. Much of this information came through during the time I was teaching, especially teaching automatic writing. I have presented the writings that would be beneficial to both the novice and the teacher. Spirits, especially highly evolved masters who are very old souls, often answer questions with a strange dialect. I have added parentheses to words to clarify the spirit's meaning. This does not change the actual way it was written.

Question: How can we be sure automatic writing is not our own thoughts?
Answer: Writing is due to feelings, but *we* (spirit guides) help.
Question: Does writing with a group of people give more energy to automatic writing?
Answer: Yes, it gives additional energy to the writer.
Question: Do spirits hear our words?
Answer: Yes, those who are near. They see the color of the person's energy and interpret those colors into word meaning.
Question: Do other spirits see humans while automatic writing?
Answer: Yes. Spirits come because they see the light emanating from the guides. Guides create energy as they work, and light appears for all to see.
Question: Is it best to first communicate with our personal guides?
Answer: Yes. Personal guides are near and give you energy to write. Spirit guides help the personal guides.
Question: Why do people reincarnate?
Answer: All earths in the universes have change. Evolution is necessary for the harmony of the universes. If you were not to change, then there would have been no reason for you to have experienced this specific life. Life experience changes a person. When a soul views (its) previous life, another change takes place. Life is change. Souls reincarnate as a way to refine their vibrations to be in universal harmony.
Question: When in regression, can we ask the image of a past life questions? How will past lives be heard?

Answer: Yes, you can mentally convey a question. The answer will not be heard as voices within the head but as thought transference. The images or time frame are transmitted to you by thought transference.

Question: Can a past life reading be done for a future life?

Answer: It is not wise for a beginner to attempt a future reading. Do not ask.

Question: Explain how to accomplish an in-between past life.

Answer: By lowering the brain waves to theta. Mentally request a past life or in-between life be seen. In-between life is usually only seen by those in knowledge of the spirit world. The average layperson might not understand what they were witnessing.

Group Discussion Checklist

Discuss the above spirit's writing.

Question: What are the images that appear as musical bands in an in-between life?

Answer: They may appear as bands of the musical scale, but they are bands of energy souls. Spiritual energy is so harmonious that it appears as bands of composed music to the human eye. In-between life is a source of true harmony. It is good to learn the importance of harmony with others.

Question: Do spirits see disharmony?

Answer: Yes, of course they see disharmony. They see it every day. They see the disharmony of those in spirit and on earth. Disharmony in the spirit world is seen. It is felt. It (does) affect. Disharmony in the physical would feel, but it attacks the physical body. That is how we, spirits and humans, learn: by our own disharmony.

Question: How does change take place?

Answer: When the conscious mind chooses to change its choice, it will lose its addiction to repetitive choices. This is a chemical withdrawal. A group of cells come in for nourishment and then move out to heal or repair.

Group Discussion Checklist
    Discuss the above spirit's answers.

Part 2—Questions Answered through Automatic Writing

Question: How is a dimension created?
Answer: A dimension is a place that one creates. We should all be in the same harmony but for our personal thoughts that divide us. Division is an awareness, a place of being. Still, we on the earth and in spirit see how each of us have separated from the universal harmony.
Question: Tell me about the soul.
Answer: The soul is you. You are *all* in a soul. It is the essence of all you are.
Question: Is the soul a personality?
Answer: It is you.
Question: Is the spirit a personality?
Answer: The spirit is your existence in lives or existences. It comes in with the soul to be with the soul. They are interchangeable. They are you. We are *all* of you. We are the spirit within you. We are not the soul within you. We are connected by the spirit of all who have come to be in any existence.
Question: Does the soul have one physical existence?
Answer: No. It is progressive. It is as you have learned; it is progressive. The soul develops its spiritual contract as it endures each physical existence. We are not your soul. We are your spiritual connection.
Question: How many lives does a soul have in a physical body? Millions?
Answer: No. Not millions, but trillions of physical lifetimes. Each is progressive. Your soul develops as your spirit. Why do you ask for numbers? They are of little use. It is not numbers but, ideally, existences of progress.

Group Discussion Checklist
    Discuss the above spirit's answers.

Part 3—Questions Answered through Automatic Writing

Question: Tell of reincarnation.

Answer: Reincarnation is your way of progressing to a nearness of the *God* consciousness. Without progression, where would you be? Yes, you do return to develop the *All* of who you really are. Yes, to be God, if you will. (The spirit of my teacher, June Black, continues the information) Yes, love. Reincarnation is a physical existence repeated to become one with the God consciousness. (June Black leaves. My writing guides return.)

Question: Do we reincarnate on other planets?

Answer: Yes, of course. We have existed beyond time. We have always been just as God has always been. However, we have existed in God, not apart from Him for all time. Now, we, you, and I, are finding the way back to God with each progressive existence. Each existence does not mean a physical life, for you and I have been in different essences (bodies) in all times since we decided to learn. For isn't this why you are here? To learn? Certainly, learning is deep within. It is not necessarily learning on a physical level. Learning is doing from the God consciousness.

Question: I have been told a person is allotted seventy angels. Is that true?

Answer: Where is that? Does one angel not do what seventy can do? Certainly, you do not understand the power of one angel. It is, therefore, not necessary to have seventy angels. But if you feel you have a need for seventy, then amen, so shall it be. Numbers of angels is not what you should be concerned with. For if you knew the power of one single angel, it would startle you beyond comprehension. They, we, you are all powerful.

Group Discussion Checklist
Discuss the spirit's writings.

Chapter 12
SPIRITUAL SCHOOL OF LEARNING

The previous material has provided you with the ability to develop psychically and regain your natural intuitive intelligence. You may have seen your guides and/or angels and are ready to experience a closer communication with the spirit world. Each different meditation has brought you to a point of understanding the next meditation.

Meditation to the Spiritual School of Learning is a very deep meditation that requires lowering the brain waves to a very relaxed state of being. While in meditation, you will receive whatever information or experience the spirit world feels you are ready to understand. Each person will experience a different lecture or message from the world beyond. Each time this meditation is repeated, it should bring additional new information. Sincerity is required to receive spiritual knowledge.

Meditation to the Spiritual School of Learning

"Close your eyes. Visualize a white light around your body. Feeling very … very … peaceful. The light is covering your body. (Pause.) Slowly take a deep breath, drawing in the God light. You're breathing slowly … deeply. (Pause.) Breathing in the God light. Use your mind to direct the light through your body. Feel the light as it flows through your body. Feeling very peaceful. Very calm. Slowly take a deep breath and then direct the light out until it surrounds your body. (Pause for several seconds.) This is your God light protection. God is light. God is love.

"Breathing slowly ... deeply. (Pause.) Going deeper and deeper into awareness. Becoming pure mind. Your face is relaxing. Your eyes are relaxing. Your chest is relaxing. Feel the relaxation going down your spine. You are breathing very slowly. Very deeply. Your arms are relaxing. Your legs are relaxing. Becoming pure mind. Your ethereal body is lifting ... lifting ... lifting ... rising. You are floating upward. Mentally ask your angels to take you to a place of spiritual learning. (Pause.) Focus your attention within the third eye.

"In the distance, you see a shimmering white building. You're drifting overhead, closer ... and ... closer. The glowing white building is below you. You're slowly drifting down ... down. You're now in front of the school of spiritual learning. The radiant building is so large it seems to rise into the sky.

"There is an angel to your right. There is an angel to your left. Mentally ask your angels to direct you to your place of learning. (Pause.) You're floating down a shimmering white hallway. As you glide down the hall, you see many white doors. One door is open. You're entering a beautiful, spacious room. The walls and ceiling glisten with sparkles of light. You are feeling the peaceful power of the God light. It fills you with love for all. You are connected to God's love. There are many people dressed in flowing white robes waiting to meet you. They smile and nod their heads to greet you.

"A male spirit in a flowing white robe comes to you. You see his face clearly. You see each wrinkle in his skin. You see the color of his eyes. He bends near you. He is giving you a spiritual message. Listen to his wisdom. Enjoy. (Pause for ten or more minutes or as long as has been agreed upon.)

"You are now ready to leave the school of spiritual learning. You are thanking the spirits. You smile and bless each spirit. You feel your body drifting up ... up ... away from the glowing white building. You are becoming lighter ... and lighter. Your breathing is getting deeper ... stronger. You're coming back to the present time. You turn to your angels and ask, 'Let me remember the spiritual knowledge I have learned.'

"On the count of three, you will open your eyes, feeling very, very, good. One. Your breathing is getting deeper ... stronger. (Pause.) Feeling very, very good. Two. Slowly take a deep breath. Coming back. (Pause.) Feeling very, very good. Three. Open your eyes."

*End of meditation.

Group Discussion Checklist
    Did you experience the serenity of the God light?
    Did you feel compassion and love in the spiritual school?
    Describe your experience during meditation.
    Describe the interior of the spiritual school.
    Did you enter a room?
    Describe any detail you saw in the room.
    Did you see or sense spirits, teachers, masters, angels, or archangels? Each answer will depend upon what you were to learn today. There is no right or wrong answer.
    Does the group agree upon any specific clothing worn by the angels or the spirits?
    What, if any, message did the spirits give you?
    How did you receive the spirit's message: as a thought or mental communication? Explain.
    Share any experience you had while in the school of spiritual wisdom.
    Did you feel a closeness to the God consciousness?

GLOSSARY

The following terms pertain to a metaphysical meaning of the word.

Alpha: An extrasensory state of consciousness reached by slowing down the brain-wave activity from 10.5 to 7 cycles per second (cps). Alpha is known as the level of awareness that uses the sixth sense.

Angel: A divine celestial being empowered with greater spiritual intelligence than a human.

Archangel: A celestial being on a high level of spiritual progression. An archangel is empowered with a greater spiritual awareness than an angel.

Aura: A luminous essence surrounding the physical body which reflects the physical health and emotional attitude of a person on any given day. An aura may surround any living person or animal.

Aura colors: Each color, shade, or hue of the aura represents a different vibratory pattern belonging to a person's current thoughts, physical health, or attitude. Aura colors change hourly and daily.

Aura (holy): A luminous essence, usually pale pink and/or pale orchid, that emanates from the human body while in the act of praying.

Aura Vibration: An energy that can be seen as waves of vibrations as it is flows from the human body. Each human thought sends out an aura vibration that represented the intensity, or lack of intensity, belonging to that thought.

Automatic writing: A method by which the human mind can receive information from a spirit through writing.

Beta: Brain-wave activity in which the conscious mind uses the five senses—taste, touch, sight, smell, and hearing. Beta is the level most humans maintain daily.

Beta (high): An extremely fast brain-wave activity that occurs when a person is out of mental control, angry, or violent.

Brain-wave activity ranging from 28 to 21 cycles per second (cps) registers as high beta on an electroencephalograph.

Body: The physical essence of a human being. There are three basic parts to a human; the soul body, the ethereal body, and the physical body.

Brain: There are two parts to the human brain.

The right side of the brain is creative and intuitive. It receives messages by symbols, images, and emotion.

The left side of the brain is logical. It receives information on a physical level by taste, touch, sight, smell, and sound. The right and left side of the brain share information to complete a thought.

Brain-wave activity: Brain-wave activity is measured by cycles per second (cps) of beta, alpha, theta, and delta. Brain-wave activity can be measured on an electroencephalograph.

Celestial: A heavenly or divine state of being.

Cell memories: Unseen cells within a person's conscious and/or subconscious mind which hold memories of the present life and many past lives.

Chakras: An invisible part of the human body through which flows the essence of life. Chakras can be seen psychically as seven masses of faintly luminous mist within the body and extending slightly beyond the outline of the physical body. For additional information, see *The Chakras* by C. W Leadbeater, published 1927 and 1977 by Theosophical Publishing House.

Changing dimensions: A spirit may change dimensions, its state of being, many times. The first change of a dimension may occur approximately thirty years after physical death.

Clairadient: A person who has the ability to hear metaphysically-beyond the normal range of hearing.

Clairsenient: A person who senses psychically-senses beyond the normal or common way of sensing.

Clairvoyant: A person who can see psychically beyond normal sight.

Cleansing an aura: The act of releasing negative energy from the body by thought, prayer, movement, or by intention. The movement of the hands lifting over the head, as if taking off a sweater, along with the intention to cleanse the aura is one of many ways to cleanse an aura.

Coincidence: A circumstance or series of such that occur in conjunction or synchronously with each other without a natural cause.

Conscious mind: The conscious mind observes daily events and reasons information with logic.

Having an awareness of one's own mind.

Dark dimension: A lower dimension where souls reside in darkness (i.e., purgatory or hell). A place where souls are in disharmony with the self and the universe. A spirit's dark state of being that may be a mentally self-inflicted punishment caused by guilt.

Delta: Brain-wave activity that produces a dream state. The state of mind where the mind sorts and reorganizes its daily experiences and then files them into the subconscious mind for future use.

Dimension: A state of awareness. There are different levels of awareness where a soul may dwell after physical death.

Earthbound: A spirit (deceased person) who is held in an earthly existence by its own thoughts or who is unable to proceed to the God light. A spirit that has not yet passed over into the God light.

Emotion: A sense of feeling.

Energy (psychic): A vibratory force created by a person through meditation or prayer. An energy force created by breathing in the God light.

Energy field: An energy that shows itself as a luminous essence (aura) around the physical body.

An aura depicting a person's body energy and thoughts.

Ethereal body: A reflection of the physical body. The ethereal body is an essence of the three parts of a human body—the physical, ethereal, and soul body.

False aura: Not a true aura.

A false aura may appear as a white glow surrounding the head and/or shoulders of a person but is only an illusion created by eye strain.

Ghost: A soul who has not completed the process of entering the God light to become a spirit.

God: A universal consciousness that unites all people, alive and in spirit, in interconnected love.

God light: An light energy that allows entrance into another dimension. A light energy that protects the human body.

God light protection: A light energy which can be created to protect the human body. The act of surrounding one's self in protection by mentally imaging the God light around the body. Light protection to be used in the psychic exercises.

Guide: A spirit (soul) who has elected or been chosen to guide a human in all matters of the person's life.

Heaven: A spiritual dimension of everlasting communion with God. A state of heavenly bliss.

In-between lives: A dimension where a soul may existence after physical death. A level of awareness that one enters, depending upon the spirit or soul's spiritual awareness.

Influence (psychic): An effect produced upon the mind or body by nonphysical action. A nonphysical action exerted by spirits or heavenly bodies upon a person's affairs and/or character.

Intuition: The power of knowing without conscious reasoning.

Incarnation: A life existing in a different time and/or a different place after physical death of the human body. One of many lifetimes.

Jesus: A divine entity that once appeared in human body. Jesus is said to have possessed spiritual knowledge and contact with God while in an earthly body.

Left hand: The nervous system of the left hand relates to the right side of the brain. When in the act of psychometry, the left hand connects to the intuitive, right side of the brain.

Like-minded: The act of being similar in thought or action. In matters of the paranormal, a person should contact like-minded people for like-minded psychic results. Like-minded spirits interact with like-minded people.

Light worker: Old souls who reincarnate into an earthly body to assist the living in becoming aware of the God consciousness. People who convey positive thought and words to others with the intention of raising the earth's spiritual vibrations. People who help change dullness of thought, to positive thought, with the intention of bringing about the thinning of the veil between the lower dimension-earth, and the higher dimension-heaven.

Meditation: A method to relax the physical body and slow down the brain waves at will.

Meditation increases mental and spiritual awareness, intelligence, alertness, creativity, stability, energy, calmness, and improves health. Meditation assists the natural flow of energy within the body.

Medium: A person who has the ability to communicate with spirits. The medium acts as an intermediary between the physical world and the spirit world.

Mediumship: The act of communicating with spirits. The act of contacting the spirit world.

Mental telepathy: Thoughts mentally communicated from one mind to another mind.

Metaphysical: Beyond the normal state of physical senses. Based on abstract reasoning, such as by the use of intuition.

Mind's eye: The mind's eye (the brow chakra) is located behind the bridge of the nose between the eyebrows. It is known as the third eye. The mind's eye is used to see or visualize beyond normal sight.

Multi-dimensional (person): A person who exist on earth and in other dimensions simultaneously.

Negative energy: It has the power to drain one's positive energy. A depressed, angry, or violent person is constantly discharging negative (aura) energy.

Paranormal: Beyond the normal. A paranormal experience is an unproven science coming from an extrasensory point of view.

Past-life: A life experienced in another body, another place, and/or another time. A past life can be sensed or viewed while the human body is in meditation. The soul has experienced many past life times in its climb up the spiritual ladder toward oneness with God.

Personal guide: A spirit or celestial being who has chosen or has been elected to guide a person during the present life.

Personal list: A list of one's personal fears or phobias. A list to document one's progress of releasing fears or phobias.

Physical body: The physical body can be seen and touched. It relates to taste, touch, smell, sight, and sound. Any physical assault upon the body is felt on a physical level as pain or trauma.

Prayer: An earnest request to the divinity. A prayer expressed with sincerity creates positive energy.

Protection (spiritual): White light or God light is the most common form of spiritual protection.

White light is used to guard against negative energy or spirits from entering one's energy field.

Psychic: The ability to see beyond normal sight, as a clairvoyant, sense intuitively as a clairsentient, and hear beyond normal sound as a clairaudient. The ability to communicate with the cosmic consciousness and the spirit world.

Psychometry: The act of reading particles of energy surrounding an object or person by touch.

Quiver: The metaphysical act of shivering or shaking as a final release of cleansing the aura. The body's natural way of verifying a truth in psychic matters.

Rapid eye movement (REM): The slight fluttering of the eyelids. A rapid eye movement of closed eyes. Eye movement which indicates a person is psychically seeing or sensing within the mind's eye.

Regression: The method by which one can slow down the brain waves to metaphysically review a past life experience. A method of moving the memory back to recall previous life times.

Reincarnation: The rebirth of a soul into a new body.

Right hand: The nervous system of the right hand connects to the logical, left side of the brain.

The nervous system crosses from the left side of the brain to the right hand, and the right side of the brain to the left hand.

Script: Handwriting, either written or printed. While using automatic writing, a change in the style of the script may indicate a spirit is assisting the writer.

Sense: To feel, perceive, or be conscious beyond the normal. To sense something that is not visible to the human eye.

Serotonin: A hormone naturally produced in the brain. When meditating, the brain produces the hormone serotonin. A natural, healthy secretion that produces a feeling of calm and happiness.

Sixth sense: To see or feel beyond the normal senses. Normal senses are, taste, touch, sight, smell, sound. The sixth is sense.

Sensory: Pertaining to the senses. Intuitively knowing.

Silver cord: A string-like spiritual essence that connects the soul and ethereal bodies to the physical body. Human life exists until the silver cord disconnect from the physical body (i.e., death). It is known as the lifeline to the physical body.

Spirit: The non-material essence of man. The essence of a deceased person who has not yet crossed over to the God light. Spirits can move on thought patterns from one destination to another as fast as the blink of an eye.

Soul: Immortal substance of man. A disembodied intelligence with a higher conscious of thought. There are three basic parts to the human body—the physical, the ethereal, and the soul body.

Subconscious: That region of the mind that is not wholly conscious of the present outer attention.

Super-subconscious: That part of the mind that lies outside the sphere of the outer attention. Commonly, most people have full use of the conscious mind but not of the subconscious or super-subconscious mind.

Symbols: Images and forms that are used to understand a message that is received psychically. Symbols are not universally the same. Each symbol depends upon the person's experience, culture, or awareness.

Synchronicity: An act of being in the right place at the right time. A circumstance or series of such that occur without any natural cause, such as, orchestrated by spiritual intervention.

Telepathic: A way of communicating from one mind to another mind without physical contact.

Theta: A level of brain-wave activity where one receives spiritual knowledge from the cosmic consciousness, travel on the astral plane, interact with other dimension, experience the existence of in-between life, and experience the God consciousness.

Third eye: A psychic center located behind the bridge of the nose between the eyebrows. It is thought to be connected to the pineal and pituitary glands. It is used to see beyond normal sight.

Thought: An internal means to judge or reason. Thoughts travel instantaneously through the atmosphere by way of mental telepathy. A thought can be experienced physically and metaphysically.

Thought patterns: A series of thoughts that move the physical body (i.e., the arm or the leg). Thought patterns are set in the mind as a means of acting, judging, and reasoning. Spirits move rapidly on thought patterns from one destination to another.

Transfiguration: A spirit or the memory of a spirit that shows itself as a transparent face superimposed like a veil over a living person's face. The faint image of a spirit or the memory of a spirit that appears to be standing beside or in front of a living person.

Trauma: A physical or mental injury to the mind or body. The memory of a traumatic incident that can remain in the cells or in the subconscious mind for long periods of time.

Universes: The whole system of created matter, such as planets, suns, and existing space.

Vibrations: A pattern of energy. Vibrations can be seen in the aura as waves or currents of energy being discharged by the human body.

Visitation: When a soul, spirit, or ghost, visit the earthly world.

Visualization: A method used in meditation by which the human can stimulate the mind's eye to see and sense images and symbols psychically.

Vortex: An opening in the atmosphere that spirits can use as an entrance into the physical world. A person's negative thoughts or uncontrolled temper can create the whirling motion and create a vortex.

Wandering spirit: A spirit who has not yet crossed over into the God light. An earthbound spirit that wanders the earthly dimension.

White light: An energy created by prayer, spiritual thought, or earnest intentions to be used for protection.

ABOUT THE AUTHOR

Marie Harriette Kay was born in Detroit, Michigan. She is a writer, author, artist, psychic, and a natural medium. She is the mother of three children. Since she was a young girl, she experienced many strange phenomena. However, at that time, society frowned upon inquiring into the spirit world, so she remained silent through her younger years.

Marie is a control medium and can communicate with the spirit world. For the past forty years, she had studied, taught, and lectured on many phases of parapsychology.

In 1970, Marie began her psychic training with Mrs. June Black, who had her training in London, England, and had also been active in the field of the paranormal for over forty years.

In 1972, Marie became Mrs. Black's assistant, and under her guidance, she studied psychic awareness, meditation, mediumship, psychometry, healing, and past-life regression for seven years. Marie's first attempt at mediumship revealed she was a natural medium and that communicating with spirits came naturally.

In 1977, following Mrs. Black's demise, Marie began teaching meditation. By 1980, she was lecturing on psychic phenomena and teaching psychic awareness and mediumship.

In 1982, Marie received a certificate of completion for The Gotach Center for Health for Healing Touch Therapy.

In 1983, Marie took top creative writing honors at Macomb County Community College for a short story, "A Day in Court." She has been published in a literary anthology distributed by Macomb County Community College.

In 1985, Marie lectured at Sterling Heights Public Library, Foxfire

Series, "How to Meditate and Turn on Your Psychic Ability." She has also lectured at Utica Library and read "How to Meditate to Turn on Your Psychic Power."

Previously, in 1960, Marie studied oil painting at Pyramid Art Studio in Detroit, Michigan. By 1980, she was teaching oil painting in the Utica school system and had sold many paintings. She has exhibited, sold, and donated painting for various charities and raised money for the promotion of local artist.